D1245983

# THE
# JACQUELINE
# SHAN STORY

*Pursuing a dream, never giving up*

By Dr. Jacqueline Shan

BARLOW

*For my children*

Nicholas and Alex, you may feel too cool
and a little embarrassed to walk down memory
lane with your mom right now, but I dedicate
this book to you, my precious boys. In your life
journey ahead, I hope you will draw as much
strength and wisdom from your mom as I have
drawn from you. You are the source of my
courage and meaning of my existence.

Copyright © Jacqueline Shan, 2014

All rights reserved. No part of this publication may be reproduced, stored in a retrieval system or transmitted, in any form or by any means, without prior written consent of the publisher.

*Disclaimer:* Efforts have been made to ensure information is correct and accurate. The publisher and the author accept no liability for errors. We take no responsibility for loss or damage as a result of a person doing something or not doing something in accordance with the teaching in the book. The manuscript is not providing medical, legal, or accounting advice, and input from a competent professional should be sought.

COLD-FX® and ChemBioPrint® are registered trademarks of the Valeant family of companies.

Library and Archives Canada Cataloguing in Publication data available upon request.

ISBN 978-0-9917411-5-1 (book)
ISBN 978-0-9917411-6-8 (ebook)

Printed in Canada

Cover and interior design by Luke Despatie
Cover photograph by Curtis Comeau

To purchase copies please contact:

Sarah Scott
Publisher
Barlow Book Publishing Inc.
77 Douglas Crescent
Toronto, Ontario
Canada  M4W 2E6

For more information, visit **www.barlowbookpublishing.com**.

BARLOW

# CONTENTS

# Introduction

One snowy Saturday in early 2003, there I was, standing in an Edmonton Walmart in my white lab coat beside a big cardboard sign. Crowds of Saturday shoppers hurried by me on their way to the toothpaste aisle. I was there to promote a product I believed in with all my heart and with all my scientific training backing me up: COLD-FX. Weekend after weekend, for hours at a time, I put to the test my entire professional reputation, not to mention my feet, by doing what I think every boss should do—standing up for her company's product, trying to sell it myself in a busy department store. When people approached me, I chatted with them. It wasn't easy. For one thing, I'm shy; for another, during those appearances at Walmart, I had decided not to let anyone know I was the president, chief scientific officer, and soon to be CEO of my company, CV Technologies. So they had no idea who I—a petite, relatively inconspicuous Asian woman—was, as I enthusiastically urged them to try a patented herb-based natural health product for reducing the frequency, length, and severity of colds, one that had been tested and praised for its efficacy by the hometown hockey team, the Edmonton Oilers.

In a few short years, COLD-FX would become a household name in Canada, shooting its way to the top to become the number-one colds and flu brand in the country. But at that time, as the co-founder of a company that developed, manufactured, and sold natural medicines, I had no way of knowing what an exhilarating, exhausting, and ultimately challenging journey lay before me.

I was born in China and grew up to become a quiet grad student who learned, because of the social and political climate, to keep her head down and her profile low. I had gone into a career in science because I loved researching, loved the long quiet days that blended into nights in the lab as everything fell away but the experiment I was working on. Yet, after coming as a grad student to Canada almost on a whim, and doing a second Ph.D. at the University of Alberta, under my mentor Dr. Peter Pang, I became a risk-taking entrepreneur before I could even pronounce the word in English.

Together, Dr. Pang and I created a new paradigm for herbal remedies using evidence-based research and clinical trials to develop our product and prove that it worked. We had confidence in COLD-FX. In a stroke of whimsical genius, we had engaged as our spokespeople two national hockey icons: the legendary NHL All-Star centre and philanthropist Mark Messier, and Don Cherry, the hockey commentator who in public was outspoken but in private was gentlemanly. They were wonderful! Picture Don

Cherry, or "Grapes" as he is known, in one of his signature plaid jackets, leaning cozily on a bottle of COLD-FX for a TV ad. Because of them and their interest in preventive health care, we quickly earned a high media profile, with an audience who was interested in what we had to say: if you use our product, it will help boost your immune system, which then reduces your chances of getting colds; and if you happen to catch one, you will feel less miserable because it lessens both the severity and duration.

But bringing a successful drug—even nature's drug—to market is a lengthy and horrendously expensive proposition. Big pharmaceutical companies take about twelve years and anywhere from $500 million to a billion dollars to success-fully bring a new drug to market. Even then, it can fail to catch on with the public.

COLD-FX became a smash success, and I went from being a reserved scientist, more comfortable hiding in my lab, to becoming a natural health pioneer trolling for mil-lions of dollars in funding, hailed as a "scientific rock star" in Alberta and beyond. As well as working around the clock both in the lab and in the boardroom, I popped up on TV shows (at first awkwardly—English, after all, is not my first language) promoting COLD-FX. Once, dazed and dazzled, I was even led onto centre ice at Madison Square Garden by Mark Messier, while the crowds yelled "Moose! Moose! Moose!" So shy was I, so conscious of being such a long way from my childhood as a daydreaming girl in Jiujiang on the shores of the Yangtze River, that I didn't dare think I knew how to successfully stand on centre ice. What if I slipped?

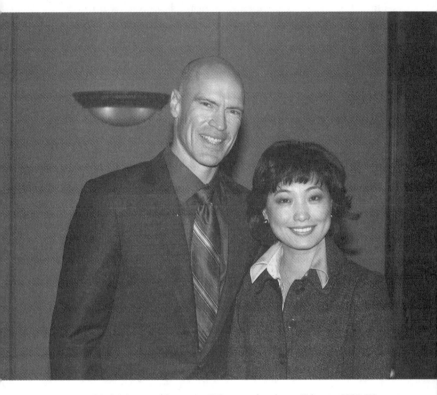

Mark Messier and me at an Edmonton luncheon, February 2007. We were celebrating the retirement of his Oilers number and the naming of Mark Messier Trail.

But those crowds hardly noticed me and my stage fright. They had a famous and beloved hockey player to cheer on.

How did an immigrant graduate student from China end up with such success? For me, it's a wonderful, improbable, entrepreneurial story with many ups and downs and not a few public disappointments. We raised millions; we invented, tested, and successfully marketed a new product that millions of Canadians swear by. But we also had our major setbacks and mistakes: advancing too quickly into the U.S. market, under a different set of rules governed by the FDA, and with a relatively young management team, some of them with little international business experience. It was a much larger and more challenging consumer landscape to deal with. Some results were painful: product returns, financial restatements, falling share prices, cease-trading orders, class-action lawsuits, bad publicity, media challenges to the efficacy of our product, managerial missteps, and a penalty from regulators that made me vow never again to run a public company (and believe me, I'm not the only CEO who feels this way). The last straw was a hostile takeover bid, started by a Canadian pharmaceutical company, which made the loss of my beloved product and company inevitable.

The company and the product were eventually acquired by another company, the multibillion-dollar pharmaceutical leader Valeant, in a friendly takeover in 2011. Even so, I felt as if I'd lost my baby. My high-wire entrepreneurial experience had made me question whether, though not yet fifty, I had what it took to start all over again. After all, I had financial security and a family to raise. Why put myself back on the front lines of both natural health and entrepreneurialism?

If I tell you that as a young girl I fell in love with one of the few North American literary heroines I could actually read about growing up in culturally restricted China—Scarlett O'Hara in *Gone With the Wind*—you may figure out where this is going: Scarlett may have been scheming and overly flirtatious (not my mode), but she was all about resourcefulness and resilience. Her favourite saying in the midst of disaster and disappointment? "Tomorrow is another day."

Tomorrow *is* another day, and I am now embarking on a new venture, in step with my cohort, as a middle-aged woman who is determined to stay vital, glowing, and healthy. I want to tell you what I've learned along the way: as a young girl in the midst of the Cultural Revolution in China, as a female scientist, as an untested CEO in a risk-filled business, and as a now mature businesswoman and natural health leader who has put years of thought, research, and personal experience into thinking about how we can stay healthy as we age.

The success of COLD-FX gave me the freedom to never have to work again, considering the relatively simple and frugal lifestyle my husband and I are accustomed to. But not working? That's not me. Being in the lab, creating good natural health treatments and products, and then figuring out how to best bring them to market is what I do naturally and what I do best. We're living in a kind of golden age in which traditional (herbal) solutions are challenging modern medical solutions to manage our health and solve our health problems. Traditional medical practices, naturopaths, and health stores are flourishing. Even practitioners of modern medicine, which has been limited to what I call cut-and-burn procedures (surgery, chemo, radiation) and expensive and often unnecessary and ineffective drugs, are becoming more open to nature's cures. More and more people are embracing natural medicines and supplements, herbs and vitamins, and essential non-saturated fatty acids such as omega-3s. They are the ones that make you glow with vitality, keep your heart healthy, and help you through life's ordinary but still challenging medical passages—like perimenopause and menopause, which I admit affected me to my core both physically and emotionally. I'm working on new products now and feeling in tune with all the other members of my generation who want to age well. My two sons are into the teenage years, my husband is a busy engineer, and I am entering this phase of my life having experienced both great success and setbacks.

Like many women my age, I'm questioning what's next for me and for my generation of busy working mothers. I'm also looking back on those early years as a woman in science. I was often insecure, and sometimes overlooked, but I now marvel at how really nothing held me back once I got going, just my own fears and doubts—and my imagination.

Now when I hire young grad students to work for me, I feel ready to tell them my story, to say, "Look, this is how you can do what you want to do. To be a scientist, you have to be stubborn. Most experiments fail. But when they succeed, they can change your life." Although unlike me, you may not end up either on centre ice with a guy named Moose or on the floor at Walmart selling your heart out!

But let's go back to the beginning, back to China, when a young girl named Xiao (little) Jie nearly didn't survive her own childhood.

# 1.

# FROM THE SHORES OF THE YANGTZE

Those sparkly little fish, swimming and shining in the Yangtze River. I wanted so much to touch them with my four-year-old hands. I was playing with a few other children, including my brother. No adults around. I reached down to grab a fish and—*oh!*—in I toppled and was quickly flushed downstream in a volatile current. I would have been that little girl, Xiao Jie, swept away to her death, but suddenly I was scooped out in a net by a fisherman looking to meet his daily quota.

This tale of how I ended up as a fisherman's prize catch became one of my family's most often recounted moments of trauma. They would say, "Xiao Jie is Ming Da." Loosely translated, it means I have a good fate (Ming) and that I will survive against great odds (Da).

During my time in the water, I had lost consciousness and had to be revived on the riverbank and carried home. After that, even without any teacher, you can be sure I learned to swim.

That was me before I knew who I was. Before I became a scientist, crossed the world, and became a natural health entrepreneur.

It's a story that is all about surviving the odds.

Like almost every immigrant story, this one starts with a very modest beginning. The middle child of three, I was born in 1963 in Jiujiang (Nine Rivers), a beautiful ancient city on the southern shore of the Yangtze River. Back then it was a relatively small, very primitive town surrounded by several rural counties and villages with a total population of about 300,000. Now it is a great metropolitan area with more than 4 million inhabitants and skyscrapers everywhere.

It's hard to fathom how independent my childhood was. Today we read about Tiger Moms (the Asian offshoot of helicopter parents) obsessively charting their children's every move. Back then? I was on my own, my parents far too busy just trying to survive in a crushing regime to worry about whether I did my homework, let alone what I was going to be when I grew up.

When I was a young child, the Cultural Revolution was underway. Begun officially in 1966 under Mao, it was an expansive and sweeping social movement that devalued individual achievement, monetary success, and intellectual achievement. It resulted in tremendous instability, forced relocation of urban workers and smart people like my parents to rural areas, and widespread starvation that left young children like me malnourished for years.

Everyone, including my parents—my mother, Shuling, and my father, Jiaren—was stressed about their lives in general. (Many men smoked constantly and my dad in later years got lung cancer and died of esophageal cancer.) My father was the oldest son in a farming family from a village near Jiujiang, with five brothers and two sisters. He had been lucky to get some basic schooling. Not much—but enough for him to master reading and writing. Eventually, in order to support his family, he went to the city and found a job as a secretary in a local government department. He was only sixteen. Young, hard-working, and smart, he was sent on various government programs in management and government policies, including law. He took on more responsibility and was promoted to various positions. At one point before the Cultural Revolution, he was the head (mayor) in Jiujiang county. Like many people working in the government, my parents experienced a lot of hardships. Mom told me that one year we moved five times by truck or by boat to be relocated in different counties. I suppose it was because Dad had been demoted. After the Cultural Revolution, we moved to the city, because Dad was transferred back to work for the city government. By the time Dad retired, he was the deputy head of the city justice department (or district attorney's office), the department responsible for prosecutions.

When I was little, I was told that I looked a lot like him. I know that I was like him in other ways too. From observing my dad, I learned early to be quiet, to be loyal, to work hard, and to keep my head down.

Jacqueline Shan

I remember my father telling me in his quiet voice, so long as you have good intentions, good education, knowledge, and a good attitude, you've got everything.

As if to counterbalance all the psychological stress, our county, Jiujiang, was naturally beautiful, graced by a large mountain and surrounded by water. All my life, I have responded to and remembered this exquisite natural beauty. It has continued to calm and inspire me.

I was a daydreamer enraptured by all that water around me. Our parents, always working or at meetings, may not have had the time to look after us, but still they sheltered us and fed us, and with Grandmother at home, we were safe and warm. It could have been a lot worse, and in fact most of the time, it was quite peaceful.

I was quiet, and not very healthy. Food rationing meant that most of the time, we—my parents and grandmother, my older brother, younger sister, and I—simply didn't have enough to eat. For our little family of six, each adult was assigned eighteen pounds of rice, a limited amount of eggs, and only one kilogram of meat for all six. I was terribly malnourished and skinny, and I felt unattractive, the opposite of a robust glowing child.

Since then, I have always loved eggs but hated the smell of meat or chicken cooking. I had a brief flirtation with meat while in university and got a little chubby as a result. But mostly, it makes me gag.

Apart from malnutrition, I also had a severe respiratory problem because everyone smoked. I think I was just vulnerable to infection. Which brings me to another childhood trauma that directly affected my scientific career: at four, I developed meningitis. When it came on, I was home with my grandmother and dad, and suddenly I developed a high fever and began vomiting. When they finally took me to hospital, the diagnosis was meningitis. There were fears I would have permanent brain damage. It took me a long time to recover, with my grandmother whipping up mysterious herbal remedies, some of them quite vile. *What are they?* I wondered. Later, when I was older, I went into the fields with her and picked herbs. Whenever I was ill, she wanted me to have chicken soup with ginseng mixed in it. Ginseng, of course, became the main ingredient in COLD-FX, but it was many years and two Ph.D.s later before I figured that out.

I also had an uncle who was a herbal medicine doctor. He lived in a village, and I remember one remedy he made—ants mixed with honey! Even at the time I thought that was pretty cool.

My entrepreneurial side might have come from my mother. Her family—she had five sisters and two brothers— had the only little grocery store in her village, and everyone trusted and respected them. Unusually, she was also educated to the junior high level since she was the eldest daughter. To help support her large family, at the age of fifteen she was courageous enough to open the first post office in her town.

I hardly remember spending any quality time (talking, hanging out) with my parents when I was growing up—they were always so busy. In summer, they were often relocated to toil on dam projects to prevent flooding. Floods often occurred in summer due to the combination of the Yangtze

River, surrounding lakes, and poorly built dams. Sometimes in summer my parents would work in rice patches full of water, planting rice shoots. It was back-breaking work and my father suffered physically. That "damn dam," we used to say. Once, a pandemic caused what was called in Chinese "blood-sucking parasites" (some type of leech) among those working in the rice patches. The serious infections caused cirrhosis—hardening of the liver—or even eventually liver failure and death. Unfortunately, my father contracted liver disease in his mid-thirties, and doctors told him he had six months to live. By some miracle, he recovered and survived this ordeal.

I don't remember my parents ever sitting down and having a serious talk with me about excellence, about my future. This failure resulted in some deep emotional pain later in my mom's life. When I was an adult, she would cry and apologize for not being there for me when I was a kid. (She really is a lovely mom, and more than made up for it, coming to Canada with Dad in 1998 when I had my two sons and was busy starting and then running my company. My parents helped me tremendously.)

Looking back, I see that being left to my own devices was not such a terrible thing. We may be far too involved in our children's lives today, measuring our success by theirs, always wanting them to "be happy" but also to get that graduate degree and make us proud. I have said to my friends that if their kid doesn't get into Harvard, so what? And when one of my boys recently said to me, a little carefully, that he thought he wanted to be a writer, I said, "Great!" He said,

"Mom, I was afraid you'd be mad. I thought you wanted me to be a doctor or an engineer."

As a young child, I soon learned on my own to enjoy school, where I was called by my formal family name, Shan Jie. There I could write endless essays about all the beautiful nature surrounding me, even without the teachers assigning the work. I greatly admired my teachers. But slowly I was getting an inkling of what lay in store for me as an adult. It wasn't good. In keeping with the values of the revolution, I knew that once I graduated from high school I would be sent to the country to become a peasant. I became increasingly desperate. But because I was already such a little perfectionist, I also kept wondering, "How can I become the best peasant?"

Now, with so many striving Chinese and a booming economy, it seems laughable, but back then, individual success was politically frowned upon.

Watching my teachers, I started thinking, *Well, they're still going to need teachers; they're still going to need government officials.* When I was about seven, in grade 2, the elementary school formed an orchestra. Every school needed one to sing and dance to, mostly to celebrate and praise the great "victories" of the Cultural Revolution. I was selected, like other kids, based on good behaviour and good grades. I learned to play different musical instruments, including the violin. It was then that I learned how to appreciate the beauty of music, which provided great comfort and a spiritual sense to me later on in life. But my natural fallback, and the way I measured myself, was always good grades. I desperately wanted to meet my teacher's expectations, to be

Me playing the violin at around age 13. Playing violin was one way for me to escape and indulge in daydreaming. Music, any kind at any time, takes me to a different world, one much more pure and joyful than the real world. Part of my dreamer's nature is rooted in hours and hours of playing violin and listening to the radio.

like them one day. Somehow, from them, I got the idea I could go on to university.

In my own private daydreaming world, the values of the Cultural Revolution somehow did not prevail, although we were taught to hate the West, to not think about material things, to do what was expected of us as workers. But one good thing was that girls were treated as equals to boys during this period, so I had no sense that being a girl would hold me back.

I was always good at my school work, achieving high marks in all subjects. For a dreamer, I had a fairly concrete mind. There has always been that yin and yang in me between science and daydreaming.

I didn't have access to many Western books or ideas, but in high school, I did read *Gone With the Wind*, translated into Chinese, and I fell in love with Scarlett O'Hara. She was so brave, so resourceful, so determined. I wasn't street smart or selfish like Scarlett, but before I was a teenager, I had already privately accepted, as Scarlett did, that anything I wanted in life, I pretty well had to arrange for myself.

By the end of my high school years, the Cultural Revolution was over and post-secondary education was once again approved. After getting high marks on the national entrance exams for all universities, I was accepted at the Shanghai First Medical College, one of the top medical schools in China, for my undergraduate study.

For me, at fifteen, that was like going to Paris. Shanghai was the most modern and industrially advanced city in China then. Even getting there was a daunting adventure — I had to take a large passenger ship alone for three days down the Yangtze River to Shanghai. Even to buy my boat ticket cost my family a half-month's income. I took with me two changes of handmade clothes, which I wore for five years, and a very old blanket.

I was terribly shy when I got there, but that didn't matter—all I wanted to do was study. Anatomy, physics, chemistry. I didn't have confidence, but I had drive. I had focus. All I could think of was what I didn't know, and how I had to learn it. It kept me up nights. I was terrified by my own ignorance.

When I was studying anatomy, I took the cadavers, those human skeletons, back to the dormitory I shared with five other classmates (many of us did the same) and went over each nerve, each bone. I memorized the whole textbook. I went a bit crazy, wondering how I could ever go to work for someone if I didn't know how the universe started. Now I know that it's unrealistic and a bit stupid to think you have to know everything before you start—you don't have to be perfect—but at the time and for many years, I simply lacked confidence. Nobody really told me "Yes, yes, you can do that." That's why, in the past ten years, I have hired young people and pay particular attention to mentoring them, to showing them that, yes, you can do what you want to, whatever you dream of.

All students in our class lived in school-assigned dormitories. Male students in one and females in another. I shared a dormitory with five other girls, sleeping in bunk beds, and we formed close relationships. My former classmates are still dear friends, accomplished and content, now living all over the world—three in the United States, one in

Me studying at the student dorm in the Shanghai First Medical College in 1981. I shared the dorm with five other classmates. It had three bunk beds and two desks.

Australia, and one in New Zealand. I was one of the youngest in the class and from one of the least advanced parts of the country—and a country bumpkin to boot. I couldn't even understand the dialects being spoken; I had no clue what the Shanghainese were talking about. I went through a tough time with culture shock. But I found a way to adapt.

I had to learn how to manage everything in my daily life, but because I was a student it was relatively simple—go to food hall, go to class, go to library, go to bed. No dating allowed.

Only recently when I got together with one of my roommates, Xiaotian (Xinia), on a memorable trip to Paris to celebrate our fiftieth birthdays did I learn that not everyone followed the rules. "What?" she asked. "You were not aware of secret dating?" *Uh, no.*

Maybe for that reason, I was a very good, unrebellious student, very focused, not into social life. I was a typical Chinese girl at the time—no makeup, handmade clothes. People back home called me an ugly duckling because I was skinny and pale when I was little. I had no sense at all of being attractive.

I majored in pharmacology and loved it. I never wanted to be a medical doctor seeing patients. I think hospitals scared me from a very early age. I wanted to be a researcher, to study the medicines and how drugs worked on human bodies.

Back in high school, I had always been in the top five of my grade, which included twenty-two classes of about a thousand students. But university was even more competitive. Just imagine, everyone had been at the top of his or her class—and they came from across the country. The quest for knowledge was everything, and of course we had no Internet, no information at our fingertips. My philosophy was "Always be good at the one thing you're doing at the time." I just wanted to do well because I thought "if I do well in this course, in this test, in this lecture, *the next step will come to me*." It always did.

That last year of undergrad was so nerve-racking. It was almost impossible to get into grad school in China, and I knew I wanted to. If I didn't, I would be sent back to my hometown, where there was little opportunity, few universities, and even fewer research labs.

At the time in China, only about 10% of students in undergraduate school were accepted by a graduate school based on the results of very stringent entrance exams. They asked me during grad school interviews what my backup plan was. I had none. So it was a good thing a minor miracle happened: I was the only one that year who was accepted as a graduate student to work with a top and famous pharmacologist, Professor Zhengan Wang, chairman of the department of pharmacology at the Chinese Academy of Medical Sciences/Peking Union Medical College. God knows how many aspiring young pharmacologists in the country had applied to be his student. For one thing, this was the top medical research and teaching organization in the county. It was an honour and I was determined to be worthy of it.

When I travelled from Shanghai to Beijing in May for my interview, I immediately fell in love with the capital city. It was much more open than Shanghai, with wide spaces, squares, and broad roads, and everyone was very welcoming.

When I arrived, I was picked up by a senior student on a bicycle with a side car. Instantly I felt so happy. The next four years were the happiest of my life.

The Chinese Academy of Medical Sciences/Peking Medical College was very close to Tiananmen Square. At the time, I was twenty-one so I was gone before the 1989 Tiananmen Square uprising event, already starting a new life in Canada. But until then, I was at the top medical research organization in China, majoring in cardiovascular pharmacology. Despite all the criticism of all things Western, we were studying Western medicine—it was science-based after all.

Herbal traditional medicine then wasn't much about science at all; rather, it was about empirical knowledge passed down from generation to generation. It was herbalist, and sometimes about your grandmother mixing something mysterious in her kitchen. Nonetheless, there exist precious pharmacopeia with thousands of years of history written by famous herbalists and traditional doctors. We did learn some formulations in one semester in our undergraduate year.

Although I was completely engrossed in science, in love with it and the opportunities to do research, I had become a little more outgoing, with six female roommates, all of

*Opposite page:* With classmates in graduate school at the Chinese Academy of Medical Sciences in 1984 (I am in the front row, third from left). Most of us came from different provinces in China. It was pretty exciting to be able to take a picture together in Tiananmen Square.

With my fellow graduate student and roommate Jingjing Tang, who majored in biochemistry, in the dorm of the Chinese Academy of Medical Sciences in 1985.

whom I found fascinating. And yes, I did finally date—I met my husband, Yuejuin (Eugene), and married him there, before I came to Canada. I proposed to him in a not entirely romantic way, but you will hear that story a little later.

In my second-last year in Beijing, an opportunity arose that changed my life. Dr. Peter Pang, a Canadian scientist and chairman of the physiology department at the University of Alberta, was looking for a research associate. He knew my supervisor, Dr. Wang, who suggested that I should go. So without knowing anything about Canada (except maybe the name Dr. Norman Bethune, and the vague impression that Canadians were a friendly people who didn't fight with anyone), I accepted.

I was off to a strange place—Edmonton, Alberta—I knew nothing about. I had no inkling this unfamiliar western Canadian city would be where I would achieve my first business success—and acquire a new name. Not Xiao Jie, not Shan Jie, but Dr. Jacqueline Shan.

2.

# LANDING IN EDMONTON WITH NO COAT

On Boxing Day, December 26, 1987, at the age of twenty-four, I arrived at Edmonton International Airport, without a coat. Don't worry—I wasn't that ignorant or oblivious to Canadian weather. Here is what happened: I left Beijing, on my first flight ever, and flew to Vancouver, but because my flight was four or five hours late, I missed my connecting flight to Edmonton. I didn't know you weren't supposed to leave the transit zone! So I did, and then of course I had to figure out a way back in. I panicked. I finally got a porter to help me. He looked at me with a certain expectation. But I simply didn't have any cash, having figured I would get some when I arrived. That is the dependent mindset, I admit, of a Chinese graduate student who has always been looked after in her simple life of library, lab, research, and study. Money? What was that for?

I was so embarrassed. I said to the porter in my terrible English, "Could you write down your name and I will send money to you?" He was quite a friendly guy, and he just shook his head and told me to forget it. He waved away my thanks. I must have looked very young and confused.

I had also left behind my only coat in the security check in a panicky rush. What was I thinking? Thank God it wasn't snowing or even all that cold when I finally got to Edmonton.

So here I was in Alberta, at the invitation of Dr. Peter Pang (I would later learn, like others, to joke and call him Peter Pan), the Yale-trained head of the physiology department at the University of Alberta. I had come with substandard English, only a vague idea of what I wanted to do (I already had one doctorate in pharmacology), and not a clue as to how or even if I would fit in with Canadian academic life.

This first day was truly a test. There was no one to greet me in Edmonton, and I wandered the airport wondering what to do. I had to ask an airport worker if I could use his phone. Finally, I got in touch with another graduate student who came to pick me up. That first drive into the city was startling. I had never seen such a blue sky. It was so beautiful. I also noticed many large open fields, and not many people. My amazement continued as we drove through more built-up areas. Shanghai/Beijing had been full of people. Millions of them. Here I didn't see very many people walking around. Here it was so clean. And the people seemed unusually friendly. At that time in China, the service system was not friendly at all—service people were often rude to customers and strangers. So the result was, whenever I went to a strange place or met strangers in China, I was often very timid and afraid of people treating me badly.

In Edmonton, I slowly settled in to graduate student life, living in a modest basement apartment near the University of Alberta with two other students. Because of my language problems and general shyness, I suffered severe culture shock.

I spent six months being pretty lonely, and all I really wanted was to go back to China. I had just gotten married and I missed my husband terribly. Whenever I heard or saw an airplane, my eyes would swell with tears. I wanted to go home. I had to admit, though, there were definitely perks: in China as a graduate student we were paid the equivalent of $8 Canadian a month. Here, I was offered $1,000 a month as a stipend! I was amazed. *Oh my god*, I thought, *I am so rich*.

The first time I went to the grocery store—Safeway—near the campus, I was overwhelmed. I had never seen food like that. I was crying, literally. I thought I'd gone to heaven. All this food, and you can pick out whatever you want! So many kinds of apples, so delicious. And the eggs … Back then in China everything was rationed; here, a dollar twenty for a dozen big eggs. I will never ever forget it.

I had to work hard at my English. The problem was that if people didn't come and talk to me, I didn't talk to them. Some people thought I was depressed because I kept my head down so much. But I was just shy, lacking confidence.

However, once I actually got into a lab, I was fine. You develop a social life there, even when you're working night and day. At the beginning, I was continuing the research work in the same field as I'd been studying in China, about how the parathyroid hormone regulates the cardiovascular system. Dr. Pang had invited me to join his research team investigating a certain type of blood pressure—raising hormone levels and how they correlate with some types of hypertension. Dr. Pang became my mentor and, eventually, my trusted colleague and business partner in launching CV Technologies, our first natural health biotech company, spun off from the department of physiology at the University of Alberta.

The lab was my natural habitat. My fellow researchers became my family until my husband, Eugene, was able to join me, and we worked and played together. I'm sure we all fit the stereotype of the nerd scientist perfectly, but the truth is, most of us loved our work and wanted to keep going day and night. When I was doing my research, my experiments were all I cared about. I only came out to eat and go to the bathroom. I could stay there for forty-eight hours straight, working out how hormones such as estrogen and progesterone, parathyroid hormone, and some research drugs like calcium channel antagonists would affect intracellular calcium on cardiovascular cells. What fascinated me was the way changes in these hormones could affect one's blood pressure. Years later, one of the research papers that I published in the *American Journal of Physiology* demonstrated that estrogen is able to relax constricted blood vessels. This

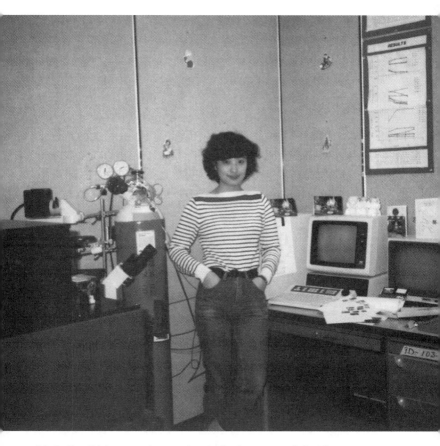

Me in Fura-2 lab as a graduate student in the department of physiology, University of Alberta. I was doing research on intracellular calcium regulation. I sometimes worked for days in this small and windowless lab. The experiment had to be carried out in total darkness because it was a light-sensitive fluorescent-based study.

was an important finding: estrogen might help to ease hypertension, or high blood pressure.

One professor I remember very well said to me one day, in both frustration and admiration, "You young scientists, you're not even human." But scientists *do* have to let their hair down now and then! Most of us loved music, and we were very into it. By then, I could listen to all kinds of music. The classics were still my favourites—Beethoven, Mozart, Mendelssohn's violin concerts—but I also liked some popular songs.

Dr. Pang, who was close to his fifties at the time, had extremely good communication skills, especially when it came to teaching. He often made very complex scientific matters easy to understood, and as I learned from him, he pushed and helped me in many ways. My first challenge: he asked me to present my paper about calcium affecting hormones at the Western Pharmacology Society's annual meeting in Banff. I was only twenty-four, and I'd never done much public presenting in English. The first time he asked me to present the paper in English, I cried. Even in Chinese I was shy, so imagine what I was like in English. I managed to present the whole paper, no problem, because I had memorized it, but when it came to the question-and-answer period, tears began rolling down my cheeks. At scientific conferences, people love to ask questions and critique, but in a panic and not quite yet mastering the listening and speaking, I couldn't understand what they wanted from me. I thought, *My god, I am going to die.* I was totally panicked and embarrassed.

Now, of course, it's much, much easier for me. I even enjoy it.

I think because of my strong sense of accountability and persistence in solving problems and completing assignments, Dr. Pang found me reliable and frequently showed a lot of confidence in me. He ran a large lab that attracted many researchers around the world to collaborate with him. He was very successful in receiving not only academic funding, but funding from pharmaceutical companies. During that time, there was much more funding available for medical research. It was also the golden era for biotechnology innovation and the life sciences industry. Pharmaceutical companies, along with venture capitalists, poured a great deal of money into these companies, hoping to discover and develop groundbreaking drugs and medical devices.

Dr. Pang had a large lab, often with almost forty people doing various research projects. Over time, Dr. Pang put me in charge of several research projects, and I had to learn how to manage people as well as evolve as a scientist.

Managing people is still a struggle for me—if a technician comes to me at the end of the day and says, "I can't finish this because I have to get home to my family," my first reaction is to say, "You go and I will finish up for you."

I have always been a non-confrontational person, more comfortable in the lab than in the boardroom. When I became the CEO of my own company, I sometimes had to find ways to argue my points, but that was half a decade away.

I had never worked at an actual job in China. I was always well inside the student bubble, where I didn't have to worry about my own survival. Personal relations were tricky back then. Human decency was scarce, and suspicion was everywhere. In contrast, I loved the friendliness in Alberta, the easy social graces of the people I met and worked with.

Eventually my husband joined me in Canada. I should now tell you the story of how I married my husband and brought him to Alberta. Because, even though it demonstrates—a bit too much!—how strong-willed I was, it also is a story of what we were up against in China and how marvellous it was to come to Canada and see that things like personal freedom could be so different.

When I was a graduate student in Beijing, I was working so hard that my girlfriends told me, "You need a boyfriend." They introduced me to Eugene—a hard-working Qinghau University graduate (Qinghau University is the top engineering university in China), and then a graduate student at the Chinese Academy of Sciences, majoring in electronic engineering. We got along very well. We hadn't been dating very long—maybe eight months—when I got the offer to come to Canada. So I surprised him. "I think we should get married before I go," I said. Pause. "Why?" he asked. "You're leaving, and I'm staying here to study."

And I replied, not exactly romantically, "I want to get married, to get that certification, so that I don't have to think about love and marriage when I go to Canada! I don't want to have any distractions." I was so young, I didn't want to take any risks. Not exactly the white wedding dream. But I did love him, and I thought, *This is the right thing to do.* He was a little more mature, more realistic than me, and I could tell he was reluctant. He just said, "How would that be possible?" I could see he didn't want to hurt my feelings. But finally I convinced him. (We have been married for twenty-five years, so my surprising and strange idea wasn't all that wrong. In Canada, we joke about the story but people who hear it are sometimes shocked: "You actually did that?")

Then we had to battle bureaucracy, because several of us female graduate students were told we didn't have permission to marry because we were students. We found out this rule applied only to undergraduates not grad students. So we kept pushing and pushing the head of human resources, who was responsible for the approvals—we were all in our early twenties and of a legal age to marry, so why couldn't we get married? Finally, after a lot of arguing, as a group, we got approval, and Eugene and I got married without a wedding ceremony. We just got that piece of paper. Then I said, "Look, I have to take you to see my parents. I have to let them know." We took a nineteen-hour train ride from Beijing to my hometown. My mom was very disappointed that I hadn't waited to have a real wedding.

While I was getting settled in Canada, Eugene was finishing his studies in Beijing when the uprising in Tiananmen Square happened. I was horrified, so worried for Eugene, and appalled it had happened minutes from where I had lived so blissfully as a student.

Fortunately Eugene wasn't affected by the demonstrations. He was able to work a bit in Hong Kong, and about a year and a half later, joined me in Canada. Just at that time, one of my girlfriends at the University of Alberta was getting

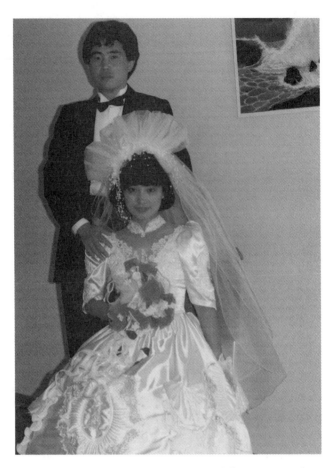

We took this picture in 1990 in our rented basement suite near the University of Alberta. Eugene and I did not have a wedding when we first got married in China. We consider this our official wedding picture. We borrowed the wedding dress and tux from our friends that evening, and took this picture ourselves using the camera's self-timing function.

married. So when Eugene finally arrived, I borrowed her wedding dress and her husband's tux (both were rented for two days) and in our little basement apartment that evening, using the camera's self-timing function, lit by a floor lamp we bought in a garage sale, we took a somewhat official wedding portrait. It came out with some dark shadows, but was nonetheless quite nice. I'm still pretty happy with it, and even though people suggested to me that on our twenty-fifth, we have a real wedding, I didn't want to make a big fuss. My mom still says, "I can't believe I didn't even have a wedding for my daughter." In China, weddings are a huge thing. But she was able to do that for my brother Kai, a then retired army officer, and my sister Ping, an engineer, both of whom still live in China.

Me? I made up my own mind, like I always do.

Some people call me focused, others boring. I think sometimes maybe I *am* a bit boring because I can be pretty simple, pretty mechanical at times. When I want something, I just do it. No big overall goal, just keep going after it, even when there are obstacles, like Chinese bureaucracy—or even my husband's reluctance. I will never give up.

When I first came to Canada and worked in the lab, everyone called me by my Chinese name—Shan Jie. My husband still calls me Xiao Jie. Little Jie.

But after I completed my second doctorate in physiology, finished the pure schooling part of my life, and was starting my business life, some people suggested I should have an English name. Easier for doing business. The name Jacqueline just appealed to me. Jackie for short. For one thing, I admired Jacqueline Kennedy Onassis. Another strong-willed heroine, but also feminine. The short form "Jackie" totally seemed like me too. I instantly felt comfortable with it. Besides, I couldn't really call myself Scarlett, could I?

3.

# ENTREPRENEUR: THE RISE OF COLD-FX

There was a time I couldn't even pronounce the word "entrepreneur" in English. Thankfully, I learned to say it before I was nominated for Woman Entrepreneur of the Year in Alberta in 2005. According to *dictionary.com*, an entrepreneur is a "person who organizes and manages any enterprise, especially a business, usually with considerable initiative and risk." *Forbes* magazine nicely refined it in a tribute to start-ups: "Entrepreneurs, in the purest sense, are those who identify a need—any need—and fill it. It's a primordial urge, independent of product, service or market."

In 1992, responding to something deep inside me, I became an entrepreneur. My mentor, Dr. Pang, and I created CV Technologies Inc., a brand-new biotech company spun off from the University of Alberta. After staring at each other in fear and wondering if we could really do this (sure we could, all we had to do was work twenty-four hours a day and raise tens of millions of dollars!), we set off together in a new direction.

We identified a need and bravely (I think) decided on a new paradigm: for the first time, we would subject a natural-based product to the same clinical trials and rigorous testing that mainstream pharmaceuticals went through. The idea of evidence-based natural remedies was a big step in the world of natural health medicine—natural remedies had never been subjected to the same kind of clinical trials as mainstream pharmaceuticals. It was also a huge and risky step for me, both in terms of money and time. There was a reputational risk too, but in science, in the lab, it's common to fail and considered great to try.

But career-wise, if you take the entrepreneurial risk and you're not established academically as Dr. Pang was, then you're going to miss that academic boat. I had to come to terms with that. It's that simple and pretty stunning in a way—I was the co-founder, responsible to others, and if it tanked, I had nothing else to turn to.

How did I go from being a busy-to-the-point-of-distraction graduate student and researcher, just completing my two Ph.D.s (one in pharmacology from the Chinese Academy of Medical Sciences in Beijing, and the other in physiology from the University of Alberta) to starting and running my own business? I think that itch was always within me. My mom's family had been entrepreneurs, even living in a country that, in their time, shut down independent businesses and gave absolutely no encouragement to those who had a business dream. Now it's different of course, but I figured, if they were brave enough to do it under those circumstances, I should be able to do it in business-friendly Alberta. Admittedly, the emphasis in that province was on oil and gas, but biotech start-ups were coming on strong.

I could have chosen to gradually gain recognition in academia and have a relatively nice home life. But when Dr. Pang suggested he and I run our own lab, I knew in my heart this adventure was for me. I was quite open-minded at the time. I was very interested in developing medicine, and I was yearning to do something tangible. If I could be part of creating some groundbreaking medicines, that would be wonderful.

Dr. Pang was one of the most intelligent people I have ever met. He was not just book smart, he was entrepreneurial smart, he was multicultural smart. He was also very open. When I was growing up, no one ever really validated me. When you grow up this way, you're always thinking, *Am I right or wrong?* That's why I am so thankful for Dr. Pang. We worked well together. I was the one actually working in the lab, on the science. He would think a lot alongside me and help me validate our concepts. Although I was young, just in my late twenties, I was pretty sharp. I just kept on learning more and more. Our dynamic was a good one. He appreciated my persistence. Dr. Pang was persistent too, but he looked after more of the business aspects and I was more into the science.

That was the start of CV Technologies and eventually of COLD-FX, which became an iconic brand in Canada. In 1992, helped by a business person Dr. Pang knew in Toronto who had established a successful biotech company in Boston, we registered and set up business plans and structures. We had around fifteen or twenty scientists on the team—I was responsible for the science—and I was pretty proud that we were able to assemble this team, find a new facility, and get the lab up and running in a couple of months. We negotiated with the university to lease a lab right on campus, not far from our original university offices. We bought old equipment from the university and hired some of the people we were already working with, and finally all the paperwork was in place.

In Dr. Pang's lab at the time we were working with several pharmaceutical companies, including Miles Canada Inc., a division of Bayer Pharmaceuticals, later renamed Bayer Inc. Miles Canada/Bayer offered us $3 million to do two years of contract research to try to find an endogenous agent to deal with hypertension—basically discovering something inside the body that would lower blood pressure. So that's what we had been working on, although we weren't successful in finding the agent by the end of the contract term.

The new company was my whole life. Even on the snowiest of days, I would be the first one there in the morning, my tire tracks making fresh marks in the snow. I would be there by 8 a.m. and stay until 7 or 8 p.m., and even until midnight if necessary. Some of my colleagues had to leave early—they had young children—and I was okay with that. Everybody did everything in that lab. I washed my own test tubes; I answered the phone in a little corner, acting occasionally as a receptionist. I thought it was fun, even though I was officially vice-president of research, the head scientist responsible for all the science. I was happy with my $30,000 salary, the most I had ever made. By the end of three years, I was making about $60,000.

I was totally content in those early days. My own company. Work work work. Toward the end of the second year, we looked at each other again. Our business partner was heading back to Toronto—he missed his family—and we had run out of money. It was a huge challenge: do we close it up or keep going? And if we keep going, where would the money come from? Dr. Pang could probably go back to being a professor, but I had thrown everything I had into the business. I was desperately thinking of ways to keep the company alive. I felt we were responsible for all our employees—they seemed like family.

We knew that if we wanted to survive, we would have to either provide a sustainable contract research service or create our own technology and products. The former is about working for other companies to create patents and discover new drugs for them. The latter is about creating your own intellectual property and assets. Either way was very difficult. In the end, we chose the second, riskier path.

Before that, though, we had endless meetings discussing what our next move should be. I said I'd like to continue— especially if we had the chance to develop a new technology and proprietary products. But we were on our own as scientists—and considering all possible sources of money. The first thing I did was to say I didn't want to get paid and suggested we freeze our salaries. We sold lab equipment, we sold off furniture, we laid off some staff. We reached out to friends and families. My husband was working as an engineer, but we weren't rich. However, I still invested in my own company with mortgages and personal lines of credit.

We approached friends in Edmonton's Chinatown, people running butcher shops and restaurants. We talked to their real estate agents and accountants and asked them to invest in the company. To my surprise, they did. We never forgot them. Later, I was able to return the favour and invest in some of those restaurants. I was very happy some years later when COLD-FX became successful and those early investors got a nice financial return. To this day, I have tremendous gratitude to our friends in Chinatown.

So there we were in 1995 with funding in place. Now we had to decide what our goal was.

In the early 1990s, nobody was trying to develop herbal medicine as mainstream medicine. We were interested in taking it on and decided we needed to focus on just a few areas, so we looked at immunology, we looked at degenerative nerve diseases, and we looked at cardiovascular disease. And all the while we were looking in these areas we were asking ourselves how we could use evidence-based practices with herbal products and commercialize the process and the drug. It was both extremely exciting and extremely stressful. No entrepreneur would tell you anything different. Innovation and enterprise are addictive drugs all on their own.

Needless to say, we also realized how important the money was, given our recent experience. You need to run a lab, pay people, fund the research and clinical trials. Consider this: the average cost of a major pharmaceutical company bringing a mainstream drug to market today ranges from $500 million to $1 billion—and 90% of all new drugs developed are going to fail! Companies can spend as much as $700 million over an average of twelve years developing a new drug, and the drug could still not succeed. If you want approval from regulatory bodies like Health Canada and the FDA, there's a stringent requirement to prove your drug, which involves many laboratory tests and clinical trials costing millions of dollars. Sometimes the company doesn't get approval. That's why biotech or pharmaceutical development and venture is highly risky but also highly rewarding if you make it to the top. Some biotech CEOs, especially those working in start-ups, can spend their entire careers, spanning twenty to thirty years, without seeing any drug they work on come to the market. Recently, one retired biotech CEO jokingly mocked biotech entrepreneurs. "Such fools," he said. I would refer to them as "brave souls," I guess, including myself.

So what is the scientific and business rationale for spending millions developing natural medicines? We pharmacologists know that the product pipelines for new chemical entity (NCE) drugs, which are the small synthetic man-made chemicals that most prescription drugs are made of, are drying up. Natural compounds, in the form of herbs, plants, animals, and earth, have huge potential. The active phytochemicals in some plants might even have therapeutic advantages over the small synthetic chemicals. They could be better at targeting complex diseases and conditions such as diabetes, obesity, and immune disorders, which are running rampant in modern industrialized societies. They have few side and toxic effects. And the majority of these natural medicinal chemicals, magic gifts nature has given to us, remain undiscovered or unexplored for their pharmacological activity.

But using clinical trials to prove the efficacy of a natural remedy is a huge challenge. Herbal products don't have just one single molecule or chemical. They have many, many chemicals and active ingredients. Do they have any reaction with the body? Can they interact with each other and have synergistic or inhibitory effects? Are some more active than others? How do you standardize and ensure consistency from batch to batch? Those are the scientific questions that, starting out, we thought were fundamental.

To deal with these challenges, we needed a way to standardize our product, and to show what was in each batch. If we could show what was in it and whether it worked, we could then tackle the huge test for any new drug: Was it safe? Was it effective?

By 1998, we had created and patented a proprietary technology called ChemBioPrint®. ChemBioPrint technology is a process that precisely identifies the chemical profile and biological activity of natural products. It is used to develop natural extracts into identifiable phytopharmaceuticals that can be standardized and patented. It was an effective process that ensured batch-to-batch consistency, efficacy, and safety. This was the process by which we could standardize a herbal remedy—kind of like fingerprinting it—to ensure the same health benefit every time. Before then, when people produced herbal medicines or supplements, one batch would work, the next batch wouldn't. In this new paradigm of preventive medicine, we were aiming to create a product that would work every time out.

To our minds, ChemBioPrint technology represented a significant breakthrough in the discovery and standardization of natural health products and nutraceuticals, opening the door to increased consumer confidence for these products. Further, this technology paved the way for groundbreaking regulatory approvals of medical claims involving natural products, offering the same degree of scientifically verifiable consistency, safety, and efficacy as that for synthetic drugs.

We decided that once we had the process of production and standardization nailed down, we needed to come up with new products and take them to the mainstream market.

In China, herbal medicine had always been a part of our health system—from generation to generation. "Here, take this," my grandma would say, handing me a bitter concoction. *Yuck.* "It's good for you!" But I never learned what was in those medicines—certainly not in my time at the Chinese Academy of Medical Sciences. They were never studied.

I don't like to say we "discovered" COLD-FX. Even for a herbal remedy, it's a much longer process of innovation and testing than that one big eureka moment.

Here is how it happened: First, we decided to focus our resources on immunology. The immune system is your body's defence system—it's like an army fighting any foreign invasion that creates body infection. For example, if you have a viral or bacterial infection, the first line of defence in the body is your immune system. So if you have a healthy immune system, you don't really need a drug because your system will look after it. Your body is like an army. It has weapons, soldiers, and generals. When something attacks your body, like a cold or the flu, which are viral infections, right away the army detects the invader. The goal of this very complicated system—your body—is to eventually rid itself of the virus. The army gets to work, wounding the virus, killing it, and then eventually cleaning it up. That's its job. Sounds like a science fiction movie.

If you have a very healthy immune system, you should not get a cold or the flu. Except, of course, that's not the way it works. Everybody gets colds and flu. Right now, you and I are breathing in germs, and our immune systems are taking care of them 24/7. But when people feel sick, whether it is with a cough, cold, fever, flu, or other viral infection, sometimes they cannot fight it, the germs are too strong, and the individual's immune system is too weak.

As Dr. Pang and I started our work, we realized there was nothing on the market that directly targeted the immune system. The anti-viral drugs that were on the market worked by trying to attack the virus. The problem with such drugs is that if they can kill the viruses, they could also possibly adversely affect other normal functions. That's why, when you take them, they come with all kinds of warnings. In addition, one of the biggest problems about anti-viral drugs is that the virus can build up resistance by mutating and changing its forms. Viruses are very smart—that is why they have survived millions of years!

In our case, we decided, the best offence is a great defence—we were all about preventative medicine, all about strengthening the immune system. This was a real departure from the modern pharmaceutical drug approach that mostly focuses on treating the symptoms. Our idea was different: use the right natural molecules, evidence-based natural remedies, to strengthen your immune system. In the body, they don't harm anything, because natural molecules that your body has been exposed to before and have proved their safety through many years of human consumption don't create any horrible and unpredictable side effects. They are targeted to identify your immune cells and help them to produce more weapons to fight a virus. In that way, they work more indirectly through strengthening the body's self-healing mechanism.

I knew there was a gap in the market for this. I had been in the field for years doing research, and as a pharmacologist, I knew there were no such drugs prescribed by doctors or available over the counter.

In the lab, we got to work extracting, isolating, and testing many herbs and other natural substances. We studied echinacea, we studied ginseng, we even analyzed chicken soup—trying to figure out why our grandmas' comforting chicken noodle soup helps soothe people with colds and flu. After much extraction and testing, we came to the conclusion that a group of pure molecules isolated from North American ginseng was our best bet. Unfortunately, you can't bottle enough concentrated chicken soup (which in China

Jacqueline Shan

has ginseng in it) to prevent a cold. But you can isolate a ginseng-based molecule and come up with a natural product that strengthens the immune system and weakens any cold virus that tries to fight its way in there.

The cold and flu remedy we developed involves one of the most ancient—it has a thousand years of history backing it up—and well-known medicinal herbal plants in the world: ginseng. Luckily, Canada is famous for growing North American ginseng, so we sourced our raw materials from ginseng farms in Ontario and British Columbia. Ginseng works on the brain and on the central nervous system and it boosts the immune system. Even the Mayo Clinic has concluded North American ginseng ups the energy level of cancer patients. However, few studies have explained why and how this herb works in the body pharmacologically and biologically. There are many phytochemicals in a ginseng root, and we don't know which chemical is responsible for which biological function in the body.

We spent years in our labs trying to separate these chemicals and test them individually on different systems— immune, nervous, cardiovascular and others. It turns out that one class of phytochemicals, a molecularly complex combination of polysaccharides, is responsible for the immune function. Another entirely different chemical group of ginsenosides is mainly responsible for the action in the central nervous system. When you mix these two groups of chemicals together, the overall outcome is that they inhibit each other. To put it another way, if you were to take the whole ginseng root or ground ginseng root or even crude ginseng extract containing these mixed chemicals to boost your immune system, unless you take loads of them, you would not get the same benefit as a small capsule containing the highly purified and concentrated polysaccharides. We needed to create a technology to extract these polysaccharides from the ginseng. They are the active ingredients in what would become COLD-FX.

We originally named this highly potent, immune-system–boosting product that we developed in the lab CVT-E002. Later we played around with different commercial names. COLD-RX? As in cold prescription? But then we came up with COLD-FX and we loved it, not just because it played off that doctor-friendly *rx*, not just because it suggested a cold fix, but because *fx* also stands for "special effects." It was kind of a magical name, which we trademarked as well. We filed our patent application on CVT-E002 in 1998 and got our first approval in 2002.

I began taking CVT-E002 and giving it to family and friends during cold and flu season. They loved it. It worked! When I took it regularly, especially around flu season, or when people around me got sick, even though I may have started to feel sick, my symptoms were less severe and the cold didn't last. We tested CVT-E002 in the labs, and it showed amazing results in boosting immune cells. We began selling it in small stores as a herbal supplement. At that time, (CVT-E002) COLD-FX could be sold as a health supplement or immune booster.

But we always knew we wanted to use clinical trials to prove that COLD-FX worked. We wanted to develop it as a mainstream, publicly accepted cold and flu remedy.

We wanted doctors and pharmacists to recommend it. When you're selling your product to consumers, they're not interested in your scientific background. They just want to know, will it work for me and is it safe for me?

The only way to get pharmacists and doctors to recommend COLD-FX was to prove, with science-based evidence, that it was safe and effective. It was what we wanted from the beginning, when we set out our vision to develop natural health products—to be accepted by the mainstream pharmacy and medical community. I did not want it to be an "alternative" medicine, which very often connotes "non-science based."

So began our decade of using expensive clinical trials to produce an "evidence-based," pure and strong, natural cold and flu remedy that would be accepted by everyone, including health-care providers.

We were moving into uncharted territory for natural health products and the challenge was huge. First, we had to show what was in COLD-FX, how it worked, and why it was successful in strengthening the immune system and weakening any cold virus that comes in contact with it.

To prove that it was effective and safe, we decided to do Phase 1 and 2 trials. We were about to find out whether the old saying "There's no cure for the common cold" was still true.

In 1998, at the University of Alberta, we collaborated with Dr. Janet McElhaney, who is not only a clinical immunologist and infectious disease expert but also a medical doctor specializing in geriatric medicine. We conducted a pilot double-blind and placebo-controlled randomized study with community-dwelling mostly retired seniors. This trial involved 43 adults over 65 years of age taking two capsules of COLD-FX for four months over the cold and flu season. The results showed that COLD-FX was very safe, reduced the incidence of acute respiratory symptoms by 48%, and reduced duration by 55%. These results were eventually published in the *Journal of American Complementary Medicine*.

In 2001 and 2002, our company made history by being the first company to prove to the FDA that a herbal product was effective. We did this in the same way that a pharmaceutical company would with a new drug—with a Phase 2 clinical trial. By then Dr. McElhaney had been recruited by Eastern Virginia Medical School, which had world-renowned expertise in flu research. Again Dr. McElhaney, along with other world-famous flu and immunologists in her team, agreed to be the principal investigator to conduct the study.

We prepared our first formal clinical trial, conducted in the United States in five nursing homes involving 198 seniors. It was a classic double-blind placebo trial, which means that some of the seniors took COLD-FX and others took a placebo, and neither they nor the doctor and the study nurse administering the pills knew who was on COLD-FX or the placebo. The trial took two years to complete, at a cost of about $3 million.

It was a huge job—a trial involves a whole lot of preparation and execution. You have professionally trained and certified regulatory experts, clinical trial managers working with the principal investigator, the lead clinical researcher, and a medical doctor. You have the study coordinator, usually a study nurse to prepare the clinical trial protocol and ensure it is scientifically sound and approved by a local human trial ethical review board and the FDA before you can initiate the trial. We needed to send professional trial monitors to the study sites to verify the study was in compliance with the protocol and that each case report complied with the study design. The process is in place to ensure good clinical practice and to meet a regulatory standard.

The completion of the trial is a very strict process involving independent statisticians, a third-party pharmacist holding the blind keys—remember this was a double-blind and placebo-controlled, randomized clinical trial—and a comprehensive computer data entry recording and management system. The final reports, including the study results, were then sent to the FDA as part of the efficacy evidence.

The trials, all regulated by the FDA, proved that COLD-FX worked. They had successfully demonstrated a significant preventative effect of COLD-FX on influenza and cold viral infections. Specifically, there was an 89% reduction in laboratory-confirmed influenza and respiratory virus infection. This major scientific milestone was a true test.

The result of that first U.S. trial, eventually published in January 2004 in the *Journal of the American Geriatrics Society*, laid the foundations for the success of COLD-FX. I felt astoundingly proud that we had accomplished what we had set out to do.

Dr. McElhaney, that wonderful world-class geriatrician, had played a pivotal role in proving COLD-FX worked in her clinical studies. I was so happy to learn later that she was recruited back to Canada by the University of British Columbia, serving as the head of geriatric medicine at the University of British Columbia, Providence Health Care, and the Vancouver General Hospital. We collaborated again later, in a much larger scaled Canada-wide clinical trial with COLD-FX.

Each subsequent clinical trial—we did more than ten—cost hundreds of thousands, sometimes up to a million dollars. Around 2002, the COLD-FX patent was approved. Even before these two controlled trials were completed, an opportunity so Canadian, so inspired came to us: a chance to test our COLD-FX remedy on a famous hockey team, the Edmonton Oilers. Here is how it happened. Glen Sather, general manager of the Oilers, was often sick during hockey season when the team was flying a lot in airplanes, and going through gruelling training and games. Somehow he heard about and used our product, and then discovered we were based in Alberta. We got together for a meeting, and the result was that the Oilers wanted to use COLD-FX. I was delighted, and then I thought, *Wouldn't it be great if we could do a clinical trial with these hockey players?* Okay, I knew nothing about hockey. I mean, nothing. And not too much about skating: I had skated only once or twice with my husband, when we were dating, on the frozen canal that surrounds the Forbidden City in Beijing. But it wasn't my skating that mattered—it was theirs. We wanted to help them skate their best, even during flu season. We arranged to give COLD-FX to the Oilers, with the blessing and cooperation of its team physician and medical trainer.

We didn't do a classic double-blind placebo trial (it was not practical at all) with them. Instead, we used diaries and tested their blood immune cells in respond to viral challenges. The immune markers measured the strength of their immune systems before and after taking COLD-FX for one month. The players were on and off planes, and more interestingly, they were stressing their bodies every day, and that's a good way to test any immune system. In short, they were perfect specimens. As their medical trainer, Ken Lowe, told the press, when one of his players got a virus it was cause for worry. Not only could it lead to more serious conditions, such as bronchitis or pneumonia, but "these guys are close-knit …. They're always together, in the locker room, on airplanes. They pass water bottles back and forth during games. If one player catches something, they can all get it."

From September to November 1998, half of thirty players and coaches from the team (the experimental group) were taking COLD-FX, while the other half (the control group) were not. Blood samples from all the participants were cultured with influenza virus both before and after the treatment period. This controlled study showed that COLD-FX was a natural immune-enhancer that allowed the players to maintain excellent health and peak athletic performance.

Word of mouth did its work, and by 2004, COLD-FX was being used by twenty-three professional hockey teams. It seemed like such a natural fit, athletes and COLD-FX.

In 2004 we did another important test to make sure there were no banned substances in our product and that COLD-FX did not induce the body to produce banned substances. That was a major concern among professional and high-performance athletes with regard to taking untested supplements. This study of the effects of COLD-FX on the doping-control urinalysis of Canadian high-performance athletes was done according to the International Olympic Committee's guidelines. To our delight, COLD-FX passed the test for banned substances and was okayed for use by the Canadian Sport Centre Calgary, an Olympic athlete training centre. The results from that study were also eventually published in the *International Journal of Sport Nutrition and Exercise Metabolism*. The centre began to give COLD-FX to its 300 athletes as a means of avoiding colds and flu, generally maintaining good health, and providing a competitive edge.

Joining us at a press conference to announce our 2004 study results was Clara Hughes, one of Canada's greatest Olympians. She was a formidable athlete, winning medals in both the summer and winter Olympics. I admired her poise, her humility, her determination. As the Canadian Press reported in July of 2004, "Clara Hughes knows firsthand the heartbreaking impact an untimely illness can have on an athlete's Olympic dream. It's also why Hughes was more than happy to participate in a news conference Thursday outlining the findings of a clinical study of the popular immune system booster called COLD-FX." Clara generously told the media: "The fact they've gone out of their way to prove to [the athletes] that it's safe is monumental."

Her support and our partnership lasted right up to the 2010 Winter Olympics in Vancouver where, at the age of thirty-nine, Clara won another medal for Canada. At those Olympics, one of the best games measured by medal wins for Canada, COLD-FX was the official supplier of cold and flu remedy for our athletes. In addition to Clara Hughes, we also sponsored other medal winners such as the charming and dedicated figure skater Joannie Rochette; Chandra Crawford, the cross-country skier and gold medallist in the 2006 Winter Olympics in Turin, Italy; Ashleigh McIvor, the first female Olympic gold medallist in Canada in ski cross; and Alex Bilodeau, who was the first Canadian to win an Olympic gold medal on Canadian soil, in the 2010 Winter Olympics. We also supported and sponsored Paul Rosen in the 2010 Winter Paralympic Games. Paul, the goaltender of Team Canada's sledge hockey team, is one of the athletes I admire most for all that he has overcome. His slogan: "Never give up."

Throughout this time of engaging with some of North America's greatest athletes, we were continually trying to raise the money to do more trials, more research. Millions were needed to keep going. It wasn't easy. While people around me complimented me on my hard work and self-discipline, it was depleting, physically and emotionally.

Back in 1996, in order to survive and raise money, the company had become a public company listed on the then Alberta Stock Exchange, which was later amalgamated with the Vancouver Exchange and renamed the Canadian Venture Exchange. The initial public offering raised a few million dollars for the company and gave us enough money to last for another three years. But by the end of the 1990s,

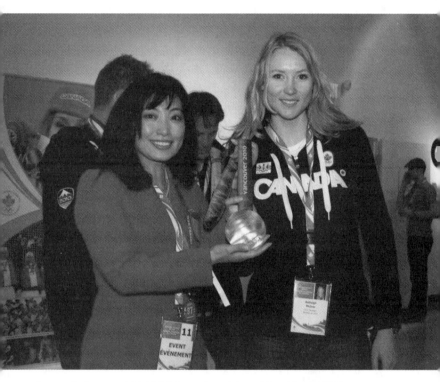

I was excited to meet Ashleigh McIvor and touch her gold medal at the 2010 Vancouver Olympic Games.

we needed even more money to survive. We had a few angel investors like Gord Tallman, a wonderful businessman and retired executive from the Royal Bank in Calgary. He believed in us almost right from the start and has provided me with great support and wise counsel.

But we were never able to convince venture capitalists to go with us—we were seen as being at too early stage, and too risky to invest in, with little prospect of financial return. People didn't understand or believe in our technology and products and the science along with them.

National Research Council Canada, through its Industrial Research Assistance Program, and AVAC Ltd., an invest-ment organization in Alberta specializing in investing in early-stage technology companies, together loaned us about $1 million to carry out some of our clinical trials. We paid them back in full (plus royalties) when COLD-FX took off.

At the end of 1990s, the company underwent many changes, as we diluted the shares and brought in more inves-tors. The original founders' ownership diminished further. It was a stressful time. There were constant changes on the board of directors and in management. Dr. Pang spent more and more time overseas and became more distant from the company. I think it was too much for him, this constant ros-ter of new investors, and new boards of directors, sometimes with drastically different visions and desires. We wrestled, for instance, with whether to stick with the one product we knew was a success—COLD-FX—or whether to develop and launch more new products. And we struggled with how to expand our market. The board of directors wanted to hire a professional business person as the CEO, someone who could lead the company through its intense commercialization phase to profitability. Dr. Pang and I were still acting like a team, but gradually as the business grew, there were more people we had to work and consult with. Eventually we went our separate ways. Our visions became different.

In May 2005, I was shocked and saddened to learn that at the age of sixty-four, Dr. Pang had been killed in a car accident in China. To honour him, we helped set up a student award in his name in the department of physiology at the University of Alberta. I wrote and published a tribute to my former mentor and colleague in the *Edmonton Journal*: "Dr. Pang, in addition to being our company's founder, was a friend, teacher, mentor and leader to many. He guided our scientists and helped open doors for success in science and business. As a world renowned scientist and enthusiastic entrepreneur, his groundbreaking work and keen vision shaped our company's scientific and business foundation. Even after his retirement from CV Technologies in early 2000, his dream continued to inspire us to pursue evidence-based natural medicine and will continue to motivate us in the future."

All through this time, I had been stepping up, taking more and more responsibility, and showing leadership in business, including pitching to potential investors and organizing product education programs for our limited distribution of stores — mostly independent health food and grocery stores in Alberta. But I also never took my focus away from advancing the product testing, manufacturing, and supporting the marketing of COLD-FX. I passionately believed that science and technology were the foundation for the success of our product, a fundamental factor to differentiate it from others. I never stopped insisting that we invest significant money into science, to provide more clinical and scientific evidence even after we became profitable. I may have had my doubts about how to proceed in business, but when it came to the science, I was strong-willed and maybe even a bit stubborn. I still felt shy about my English skills. But I discovered I loved talking to potential investors, and I would get a sense of satisfaction because people seemed to be genuinely interested in my science. And I enjoyed showing them our lab, introducing them to our researchers, and describing our techniques and scientific results. I gradually became better and more confident at communicating complex science, putting it into laymen's terms. People would praise me for what they called my "authenticity" but I still worried about my English! (My sons still correct me.)

In most cases, probably about 90% of the time, the potential investors turned us down. Of course that hurt, but you try not to take that personally.

They turned us down because what we were doing was pioneering. There was no mature business model for them to grasp the business future of all this natural health science. In a way it was easier to convince people to just believe in me and in my vision of natural products. These were people who were not trying merely to get their money back tomorrow. I think I did a good job of getting them to believe in our vision.

We were also looking for strategic alliances and were talking to big health and pharmaceutical companies to license our ChemBioPrint technology and to invest money to co-develop our products and hopefully do marketing and sales for us.

I travelled, sometimes alone and sometime with my team, all around the world to knock on the doors of big international billion-dollar companies such as Johnson & Johnson, Bayer, Unilever, and Procter & Gamble. You name it. Multibillion-dollar blue-chip pharmaceutical companies are not known for risk taking or rushing in to uncharted and what are seen very often as unproven areas such as natural health products and herbal medicines.

Those trips were exhausting, frustrating, and very discouraging. One time, to save money, I booked a very cheap motel online near New York City to meet with one of the big companies. I ended up not able to sleep the whole night because of the loud noises, even knocks on my door, perhaps by some random drunken people, not to mention the strong smells of someone smoking cigarettes. Next morning, I rushed to the meeting red-eyed and exhausted, and emerged dejected by the end of the meeting. So much for the glamorous life of a company co-founder. These trips and meetings took enormous effort from me and the company without accomplishing very much. However, throughout all the presentations, negotiations, and interactions with these international giants, I learned a great deal about business negotiation and running a business on a much larger scale.

I did have a very proud moment in 2000. After much negotiation and a very determined presentation on our part, DuPont Consumer Health became interested in our technology. They gave us $1 million to use ChemBioPrint technology to conduct a comparison study of 200 natural health products purchased from the market. This would take place as a sort of test while we were negotiating a partnership agreement. We would prove not only that the technology worked, but that without a technology like ChemBioPrint, natural products stood an overall poor chance of achieving consistency and efficacy. Leading our research team, I was commissioned to give them a thick binder full of testing results with all kinds of graphs and charts showing that, indeed, our technology worked. The larger partnership deal eventually fell through due to DuPont's directional changes. We all felt badly, most of all me, but I had gained more experience and confidence dealing with multibillion-dollar international giants, which came in handy in subsequent years.

In 2003, we launched a landmark clinical trial in collaboration with a prominent professor and researcher in nutritional science at the University of Alberta, Dr. Tapan Basu, and a medical officer of health at then Capital Health, Dr. Gerry Predy. A population of more than 300 healthy adults with a history of recurrent colds and flu were recruited and given COLD-FX for four months. This was a double-blind, placebo-controlled, and randomized clinical trial, the first trial on this scale with a natural health product in Canada. The trial went on for the whole flu season, and results came out once again confirming the safety and efficacy of COLD-FX for reducing the frequency, severity, and duration of colds and flu.

These results were later published in the *Canadian Medical Association Journal*, considered one of the top five general medical journals in the world. The trial demonstrated a 56% relative reduction in recurrent colds and flu, and a decrease in the average number of colds and severity of symptoms among healthy adults. This publication further strengthened our scientific profile and attracted serious attention from internationally respected researchers and physicians. The results were selected as one of the world's top twenty-five significant advances in dietary supplements research by the U.S. National Institutes of Health in 2006. We finally had our breakthrough.

At the very beginning, when I thought of launching this trial with a prominent nutritional researcher and medical doctor, I knew in my heart this would be not only scientifically significant, but also important enough to bring out the mainstream media's attention. I knew all along through years of research and testing and personal testimonials that COLD-FX was the best, a one-of-a-kind natural medicine for colds and flu. For one thing, I have never failed to convince anyone to take the product. They always liked it and stuck with it for one good reason: because it worked for them. I knew if we could manage to get the word out to mass consumers who would give the product a try, they would try it again. COLD-FX would become a best-seller. That is not arrogance; it is simply the logic of any business instinct: when you have the best product, when you try your darnedest to let people know, then you've got a viable business.

Yet despite all the scientific promise, we had a serious cash-flow problem. We were spending a lot of money on trials, but as of the summer of 2003, the sales weren't paying all the bills. We had only six full-time employees left; my science team was downsized to one person. We had relocated several times because of the downsizing, and we could not afford the lease on the labs and offices. Without money to pay the lab lease, we were even forced to leave our scientific equipment behind. Imagine, taking tools away from a mechanic. Letting scientists and research labs go had been heartbreaking for me, and I had to do it several times during those early years. Amidst this severe cash-flow problem, we were trying to find yet another CEO—I was the president and chief scientific officer then—and a slew of CEO candidates were marching through the company's revolving door. I counted six of them in three years. Imagine the chaos and disruption, let alone the financial loss the company had endured—it was costing an arm and a leg between signing up and severance pay when they would depart after a short stay. There was little money for marketing and little money for keeping the company going without new investors injecting money. The board of directors was determined to find a professional manager with strong skills and experience in marketing and sales.

The board did not see me as the natural choice. I agreed; I never wanted to be a CEO. Yet between the revolving doors and searching, the board asked me in the summer of 2003 to take on the title of interim CEO. During this "interim" period, I decided to publicize the launch of the pivotal clinical trial. I wanted to make a big announcement with a press conference. It was a bold move because I had never even attended or run a press conference before. I had seen these big events—either on the part of government or big corporations—only on TV, so I knew I would need help with this undertaking.

The first step was to hire a consultant with media communication experience. The consultant we found liked our story and believed we could pull off a press conference. He said he would call various media outlets. Our aim was to have the major daily newspapers and TV stations report this clinical trial as important news. We sent out our news release. On the morning of September 24, 2003, we held the press conference in the conference room of Capital Health. I, being the spokesperson for the company along with our collaborators, announced the launch of our clinical trial and answered many questions from attending media, including some medical reporters.

What happened next was almost shocking to me. The consultant called me the next morning. "Go get a copy of the *National Post*," he told me. "We made the front page." I grabbed a copy and with pounding heart saw the headline: "Trials to Begin for Natural Cure."

I was walking on a cloud. The next few days were a whirlwind of media interviews. *Canada AM* wanted a live interview in the morning. Because of the time difference from Toronto, I had to be interviewed at 4 a.m. in our lab in Edmonton. I was wired with a mike, with a camera person in the lab, and talked to the interviewer in Toronto. It was my first live remote TV interview. It turned out nicely. I then did interviews with the CBC, CTV, and various radio stations in Edmonton. The schedule of these interviews was intense, but I was so excited, so pumped, that adrenaline was not a problem. It was my dream come true, as a scientist and as an entrepreneur, to tell the story of our wonderful product, our clinical trials, and our study with the

Edmonton Oilers, which everyone seemed to love to hear about. I felt people were genuinely interested in our story. And of course, we brought our products and passed them around to the reporters and station staff—they needed to be healthy and have good voices. In a matter of a few weeks, the company saw its share price go up from about 15 cents to 90 cents. Many retail customers began calling us because consumers had started asking for the product.

The company's fiscal year ended September 30, 2003, on a high note, especially in those last few days. It was a major turning point in our history. That was the beginning of the golden era, the "hockey stick" growth of CV Technologies Inc., and the iconic rise of COLD-FX.

The next month, October 2003, the board named me as the president, CEO and chief scientific officer (CSO). I was really out of my lab coat now—the head of a fast-growing and attention-getting company. People would ask me, in person and in media interviews, "With the scientific background that you had, what was the transition like from CSO to CEO?" My answer was that it seemed like a natural move. Now not only was I involved in the creation of the technology of the product, but I was leading the company and delivering the product into the consumer's hand. But privately, I knew it was a huge undertaking.

By the end of 2004, we had our first profitable year. Over 4,000 Canadian pharmacies, food, and health-care stores were stocking and selling COLD-FX. Our sales increased 800% over the prior year, from $1.5 million to nearly $6.5 million, then $32 million in 2005 with a net profit of $10 million, and over $40 million in 2006.

By the end of 2005, as we summarized in our 2005 annual report, "there were one thousand stories or mentions of COLD-FX in the media, reaching an estimated 20 million Canadians and Americans. More than 70 daily Canadian newspapers have reported on COLD-FX, more than 100 radio stations promoted COLD-FX as part of a winter giveaway program, with many of the stations interviewing Dr. Shan." I was given the glossy cover-story treatment in magazines such as *Profit* and the Globe and Mail's *Report on Business Magazine*. The company was selected as the top-performing company in the TSX Venture exchange. Both I and the company received many awards. This overwhelming recognition ramped up public awareness and solidified our position as a leader in the natural health industry.

By 2005, COLD-FX was ranked as the top-selling cold and flu remedy in Canada, according to ACNielsen MarketTrack Drug Service for Cold Remedies, Natural Supplements, and Vitamins, which tracked all sales channels of dollar sales for the categories of cold remedies (including antihistamines) and supplements and products. We had done the impossible, and people everywhere were starting to take notice, calling us a biotech "super star," studying how we—a small natural health product company—had done it, taking on giants like Tylenol to become number one in the colds and flu category in Canada. In 2005, our brand COLD-FX was awarded Marketer of the Year by the popular industry magazine *Marketing*.

On the cover of *Bio Business* in March/April 2007, there was my picture, with these words underneath: "Inspiring a

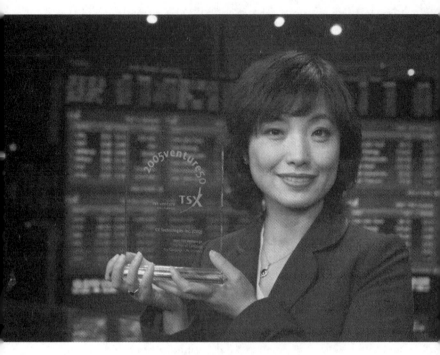

On December 6, 2005, my company was named the top-ranked company on the 2005 TSX Venture 50, the first-ever ranking of Canada's top emerging public companies listed on the TSX Venture Exchange.

nation, CV Technologies' Dr. Jacqueline Shan on her winning blend of marketing and science."

In March 2006, the company graduated to the mature Toronto Stock Exchange and began to trade under the symbol CVQ. On the first day of official trading, we had a big celebration at the Toronto Stock Exchange office in Toronto. I was one of the first women CEOs in Canada to found a company and take it public on the Toronto Stock Exchange. In December 2006, I was inducted into the Canadian Healthcare Marketing Hall of Fame—I still could not believe it, that I, a scientist, could receive such an honour in marketing!

Once we had enough money flowing in from sales, I hired back many of the scientists I had let go during the cash-strapped years. We also built a beautiful building with modern labs and a cutting-edge research facility. In retrospect, it appears to have been a steady roll-out, but of course behind the scenes, it was my own version of *Eat, Pray, Love*: try, fail, sometimes succeed, look for money. Repeat process. When it came to COLD-FX and the science, marketing, and search for sources of funding, I had tremendous will, tremendous push. I strongly believed that by advancing science, we would advance our business. In an industry that didn't always enjoy a good reputation due to lack of science or poor science, it was our investment in a rigorous evidence-based scientific approach that differentiated us from others.

I continued to believe that the success of COLD-FX lay in its uniqueness, a one-of-a-kind product resulting from

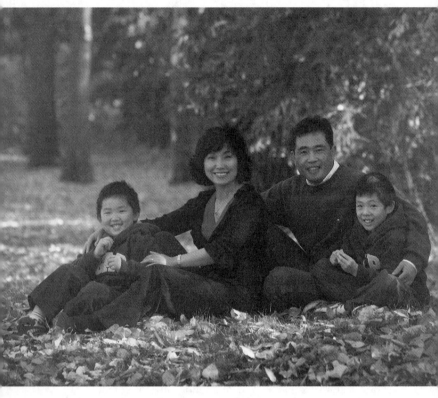

My family in fall 2006, *from left to right:* Alex, me, Eugene, and Nicholas.

years of research and trials. Its success was not gained by merely beating out its competitors.

A word about competition: ever since I was little, I have hated to compete. Strange, right? I avoided competition. I was little, I was shy, I was not athletic, and I did not believe I was very smart! I created my own little world in which I would not have to compete or compare myself to anyone else's standard. Competing with others is stressful and exhausting. It turns out that my reluctance was not bad a thing for my life and business. When we were building great media buzz about our brand, quite a few companies viewed us as a competitor. After all, COLD-FX had created a totally different landscape in the over-the-counter natural health products industry in the Canadian market. The sales of COLD-FX dwarfed the combined sales of hundreds of items from many well-established natural health products companies.

Some of them openly challenged us in their news releases to compare their ginseng product with COLD-FX. Each time, my communications staff and my scientists would get ready to fight and ask to meet the challenge. I would say no because I did not see them as our true competitors. Our product was totally different and innovative and I wanted to stay that way. I refused to make public statements comparing ourselves to others. I wanted to make competition totally irrelevant. To be good, you do not have to put other people down.

Several imitation products surfaced. You have to feel flattered in some way when people are copying you. Of course, sometimes action had to be taken against clearly illegal knock-offs. After all, COLD-FX is a patented product and is not like generic ginseng products. Most of them are simply ground-up or crude extractions from ginseng root with no therapeutic benefit or efficacy.

After COLD-FX became the number-one-selling brand in the colds and flu category in Canada, I came across a business book called *Blue Ocean Strategy: How to Create Uncontested Market Space and Make the Competition Irrelevant*. I was amazed, after reading it, that the "blue ocean" strategy was what I have believed and executed all this time in creating and building COLD-FX to be the top-selling brand. *Blue Ocean* showed how a company could create new demand in an uncontested market space. The author coined this term and made it so easy to understand. No sharks allowed! All along, I did not want to create a "me–too" product, and I did not want to compete with the top guy or any guys in the industry.

Avoiding confrontation has served me well in business. My solid education, research training, creative thinking, and determination helped me to create and innovate. I recommended the book to all my business managers and scientific team and talked about it in many of my presentations.

I was a member of the Young Presidents' Organization (YPO) and went to New York City to attend an inspirational leadership training and education event at several of their meetings. Many world business leaders and authors spoke: Renée Mauborgne, the co-author of *Blue Ocean Strategy*; Jack Welch, former CEO of General Motors; James Collins, author of *Good to Great*; and Malcolm Gladwell, author of *The Tipping Point*. These lectures were not only revealing and educational, but more importantly, they helped me build my business confidence. By listening to them, I also felt somewhat validated in what I had been doing: guided often by my intuition, I found that more and more I loved business. Business is like art, there's a great beauty about a well-run business. You can run a business in so many creative and innovative ways—there is just no limitation.

There is also science in business. I learned to lead the company, not only in the front, but sometimes from behind the team. In May 2006, I was selected as a fellow and completed a "Quantum Shift" program with the Institute for Entrepreneurship from the Richard Ivey School of Business at the University of Western Ontario. It gave me a chance to be inspired by fellow entrepreneurs and business leaders. Two years later, in June 2008, I completed the Directors Education Program run by the Institute of Corporate Directors and developed by them and the Rotman School of Management at the University of Toronto.

Expanding my business education kept me focused on our core business in the middle of all the media frenzy. I further built our brand by implementing innovative pharmacy and health professional education programs, which were very rare for the natural health and supplement industry in Canada. I built, trained, and oversaw a small team who became responsible for communicating with and educating health professionals about our company's technology and the science behind our products. The team talked to trade and health professionals and appeared at trade shows and conferences and went out on retail calls. This approach helped to differentiate our product from other commodity-based products such as ground-up generic ginseng products.

Gaining third-party validation within the pharmaceutical industry, sports world, and medical profession had further increased the credibility and acceptance of COLD-FX. Deep down in my practical, grounded heart, I knew the media frenzy would die off—if it could build you up, it could certainly knock you down as well. I knew the science and quality of the product was the true foundation for a lasting health product brand. I personally made a great effort to direct the research program and also give guest lectures and seminars in schools of pharmacy, nutrition science, and medicine in universities, sharing my expertise in pharmacological clinical studies of natural health products and the standards of quality. I went to drugstores to talk to pharmacists and spoke at scientific, medical, and pharmacy conferences about our research findings, organizing international scientific forums to which we invited scientific and medical experts from around the world to review and give guidance on our research.

I guess all these efforts paid off. COLD-FX soon became the top product recommended by pharmacists, according to *Pharmacy Post*. COLD-FX was included in the 2007 issue of the *Physicians' Desk Reference*, used by the majority of approximately 800,000 American doctors and commonly found in hospitals and pharmacies in the United States. The Canadian Council on Continuing Education in Pharmacy also approved a continuing education course ("Evaluation of the Prevention and Treatment Options Currently Available for Community Acquired Respiratory

Infections"), which was delivered to 22,000 pharmacists in Canada. A similar course was approved by the College of Family Physicians Canada and delivered online and at the annual national conference of the College of Family Physicians in October 2007.

In my letter to the shareholders in the 2005 annual report, I wrote: "Hundreds of thousands of people are embracing our vision and regularly use our products. We are confident that as the months and years go by, millions of people will hear our story and support our mission of developing and promoting evidence-based, safe and effective medicine for disease prevention and health maintenance. As the president, CEO and chief scientific officer of your company, I am also extremely happy to see that our shareholders' value is significantly increased. Our business is for a great cause and as a result, our company's future potential is really unlimited."

We were riding high, with coveted media recognition for our product. Peter Mansbridge—a huge hockey fan—even announced the success of one of our clinical trials on *The National*. Everywhere I went, I heard well-known people gushing about COLD-FX: opera singer Michael Burgess, singer Sarah McLachlan, actor Sandra Oh, and several ballet dancers. Even Rick Mercer, Canada's beloved comic, gave COLD-FX exposure on his TV show. Did I mention that Clara Hughes had declared COLD-FX "a godsend"? Each time, I personally thanked them for using our product and for spreading the word.

In the summer of 2004, we had begun an amazing partnership with Don Cherry, Canadian hockey's most famous commentator. Don was the king of all product spokespeople. In the period 2002 to 2004, our sales were generated mostly from western Canada, especially Alberta, where the company was located. I was trying to come up with a fast way to expand across the country and working with a celebrity spokesperson seemed worth trying. Our senior vice-president of Sales and Marketing, Norm Oliver, had heard that Don used COLD-FX. During the 2003 Heritage Classic outdoor game in Edmonton, Don's on-air partner, Ron MacLean, told Norm that "Grapes," as Don was called, loved our product. He then arranged to send some product to Don after the game, and Don called back within a few days, thanking him, saying he loved the product and was thrilled to learn that it was from a Canadian company. I immediately got thinking. What about a partnership with one of Canada's most famous and popular celebrities? We had several discussions over time with Don, and eventually we met with him in Toronto to explore a way to work together. The first time I met him, he told me he'd had asthmatic bronchitis when he was young and often got colds as an adult. He had suffered for many years with colds, which made him miserable. He had heard that the Oilers and Glen Sather were using COLD-FX, so he tried it and it worked for him.

In July 2004, Don became the official spokesperson for the COLD-FX brand. Don never let us down, and was the ultimate word-of mouth-brand ambassador. At the end of 2004, at our AGM, in the presence of then Alberta premier Ralph Klein, I delivered a cheque for $100,000 to Rose Cherry's Home for Kids, a charity founded by Don and his daughter Cindy Cherry. It was named after Don's late wife, Rose. Don was fantastic, and together we had a lot of fun building the brand and helping Canadians. My favourite image on print and TV ads shows Don in his famous plaid jacket leaning cozily and confidently on a bottle of COLD-FX. It made me so proud.

Don was gentlemanly and respectful to me, always calling me "Dr. Jackie." So lovely. So well-mannered. Yes, Don Cherry. He may have been gruff, outspoken, and controversial in public, but Don was always supportive and gentle to me and my staff. In public, people swamped Don, and he always made time for them. Even in the middle of a meal, he would stop, shake hands, and chat with people, no matter who they were—taxi drivers, hotel doormen, hotel guests, waiters and waitresses, airport security guards, army officers. He would take photos and sign photos at their request and ask about their families. I saw how humble he was in person. I appreciated how he defended me in public once in a media interview: "Dr. Jackie came to Canada with only $5 in her pocket ..." I was actually penniless ... but you get the point. Even though I am not good talking about hockey, we got along well. Don is a very health-conscious person, so we discussed family, health, exercise, and health supplements.

Don was always a good sport. One year, we needed help to recruit clinical trial volunteers when we were launching a multi-city double-blind and placebo-controlled trial in Edmonton, Toronto, and Vancouver. It was a large clinical trial needing 780 study volunteers, so Don went to Toronto's Sunnybrook Health Sciences Centre with us. He received a flu shot from Dr. Andrew Simor, Sunnybrook's

*Top:* With Premier Ralph Klein and Don Cherry at the company's AGM on March 3, 2005. *Bottom:* We gave a cheque for $100,000 to Rose Cherry's Home for Kids charity. *From left to right:* Norman Oliver, me, Cindy Cherry, and Don Cherry.

chief of microbiology and infectious diseases, one of the principal investigators in the trial and also walked around Sunnybrook to visit veterans in their rooms. Next day, the picture of Don receiving a needle from Dr. Simor with a grin and his signature thumbs-up appeared in the newspaper. "I didn't feel a thing when he plucked that needle in," he joked with us later.

Two years later, this trial, with an objective to examine the efficacy of COLD-FX in providing added protection to the flu shot in the prevention of acute respiratory infection in community-dwelling seniors, showed COLD-FX significantly reduced the incidence, duration, and severity of symptoms. It showed COLD-FX was complementary to the flu shot and had an added protective effect with flu shots.

Don was there for us in bad times, as well as good. I will never forget the time, when the company was financially under fire and drawing criticism from several quarters, Don called me to offer support. I was driving in the car with my two boys, and there was the familiar Don Cherry voice saying over the car speakerphone: "Jackie, they only go after the strong, successful ones. They only go after you when you're number one."

That made me feel so much better, and the fact that my sons were impressed that the famous Don Cherry had called me in my car didn't hurt either.

Don and I also began a "Salute to Hockey Moms" initiative, a national event that ran for three years to help build our brand. I came up with this idea because I was a hockey mom myself, knowing the real heroes behind all hockey players—from peewee to NHL—are their parents. Don spent a lot of his time with his grandson and very much supported the idea that we'd like to show respect to hockey moms. We launched our Salute to Hockey Moms event in five major cities. The reaction to each event was overwhelmingly positive—hundreds of moms and their hockey players, son and daughters, came to the event and told their hockey mom story. Each time, I would also speak as both the leader of the company and a hockey mom. Mark Messier also happily led one of the hockey mom events in Winnipeg in 2008. Mark talked about the importance of his mother and recalled how their bond was formed during drives to and from the hockey arena when he was younger. That day, Manitoba premier Gary Doer proclaimed September 24, 2008, officially as "Hockey Moms Day."

We had hired hockey superstar Mark Messier in June 2006, to promote COLD-FX in the United States. I admired Mark in so many ways—a great centre and captain on the Oilers, Canucks, and New York Rangers; a leader; a philanthropist; and a gentleman with great family values. He worked very hard and was always full of energy when we worked together. He was genuinely interested in staying healthy and helping others to improve their health. On one of my trips to New York, he took me to one of his philanthropic initiatives, Hackensack University Medical Center in New Jersey, where a whole building and play area bearing his name was built for children with cancer. At the Mark Messier Skyway for Tomorrow's Children, Mark had transformed the skyway into a hockey fantasyland, complete with interactive videos, games, and personal memorabilia marking some of his most memorable NHL milestones for

Mark Messier visiting our lab in March 2007. He pretended to be a "mad scientist." Mark was very interested in our research programs.

the kids to enjoy. Mark walked around greeting some of the children—I could see he was genuinely interested in them.

Knowing how important science and clinical studies were to our business, Mark helped us make connections with the hospital's infectious disease and immunology experts, with whom we collaborated and did another clinical trial on COLD-FX, this time using the doctors, nurses, and workers in the hospital.

Being around Mark was very exciting. For one thing, he and his entire family loved COLD-FX, its story, and the science behind it. He visited our lab, talking to our scientists and jokingly pretended he was a scientist. He listened intently to learn the science of COLD-FX, how it worked on the immune system. When I explained to him how COLD-FX activated the immune cells, serving as a first line of defence against viral invasion, he thought for a moment and said to me, "You mean it works on immune cells to form a firewall ?" I replied, "Yes, exactly!" How clever and appropriate of Mark to use immune "firewall" as a layman term.

Once, on the spur of the moment after a day of meetings and dinner in Chicago, Mark asked Norm and me if we wanted to go to a playoff game in North Carolina the next day. We did, so we innocently asked him which airport we should reroute our tickets to. He told us to just be ready in the hotel lobby at 6 a.m. He drove us out to the airport and to a private area, where we jumped aboard his private plane, and with Mark and his family we flew to that playoff game in North Carolina. What a thrill. It was Game 5 of the Stanley Cup finals with the Edmonton Oilers and

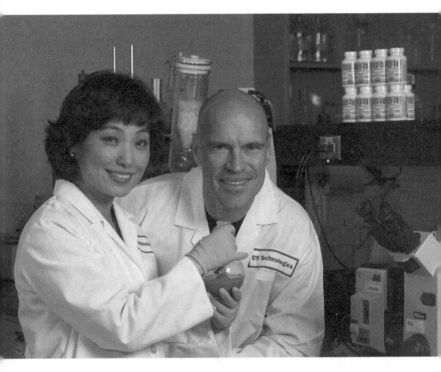

With Mark Messier in our lab, March 2007.

Carolina Hurricanes! I enthusiastically put on an Oilers jersey, ignored a few boos from the audience, and cheered for the Oilers. Too bad they lost this crucial game, but I was still proud of them for making it that far. Mark even arranged for me to ride on the flight back to Edmonton with the Oilers that same night.

But it was another encounter with Mark in New York that sticks in my mind. I was attending a hockey game with him that night. Apparently my people and his had discussed the possibility of me appearing with him on the ice at Madison Square Garden. But wrapped up in the entrepreneurial bubble (sales, contracts, science, work), I typically hadn't been paying attention to what they were planning. Suddenly, during the intermission, Mark turned to me and said, "Okay, Jackie, time to walk out to centre ice with me." I froze in fear. I was terrified I would slip and fall on the ice. But who can say no to Moose? He was so beloved by the New York fans. So I walked out and stood there, awed as the crowds cheered the great Mark Messier with his nickname: "Moose! Moose! Moose!" I thought for a moment they were saying "Boo! Boo! Boo!" to me. But they didn't even notice me. It was Mark's moment, and I was just dazzled to have been included. That's where a great Canadian cold remedy can take you. Right to centre ice.

I didn't know then, that even off the ice, I was about to slip and fall in other ways.

4.

# SUCCESS AND SETBACKS

When ACNielsen named COLD-FX the number-one cold and flu brand in Canada in 2005, we were delighted. Our share price rose accordingly, and we were riding high on new plans. Hockey players were singing our praises, and even Canadian novelist Margaret Atwood proclaimed she and her political opposite Don Cherry had "only one thing in common—COLD-FX." She didn't want her quote used for promotional purposes, but how could I not love it? Of course, I respected her wishes, and I cherish a great picture she posed for with me in 2011 at an award event, Canada's Most Powerful Women, sponsored by the WXN Women's Executive Network.

Everywhere I turned, consumers told me COLD-FX had worked for them. It made me so thrilled and proud of what we had achieved. The strangers I met in airports and on the street told me and are still telling me how much they like COLD-FX, that it works for them. Even once criticism

With Margaret Atwood at the Canada's Most Powerful Women award ceremony organized by the Women's Executive Network in 2011. Margaret was the keynote speaker and the winner in the Arts and Communications category. I was a winner in the category of Trailblazers and Trendsetters.

of the product had started, people told me, "I don't care what they said in the media, COLD-FX works for me and my family, I thank you for that." This never failed to lift my spirits and always became the highlight of my day. In the end, this is what it is all about—the guiding principle in my scientific and business life. All the hard work and sacrifices are worth it when my health product has not only been tested in the lab and clinical trials, but validated in the real world by millions of people. What could be more satisfactory for a pharmacologist and physiologist and a natural health product developer? These validations always pulled me back in the darkest days when things began to go wrong. They enabled me to get back to what I loved to do: develop the best natural medicine for people to improve their lives.

In the early days of our great success, in 2005, I won Ernst & Young's Alberta Entrepreneur of the Year award and was a finalist for the National Entrepreneur of the Year, which was eventually won by Bill Comrie, who is one of the most respected and admired entrepreneurs for his success in building his furniture empire, The Brick. After his acceptance speech, I went up to him to congratulate him and introduce myself. To my surprise, he pulled a small plastic bag full of the familiar white pills from his breast pocket and said, "I am so happy to able to meet you in person—see, I have to take these COLD-FX pills with me all the time. It really works!" He then called his financial adviser over and asked him to set up a meeting with me, because he was interested in investing. This kind of support meant a great deal to me.

With Bill Comrie at the 2004 Ernst & Young Entrepreneur of the Year award ceremony. Bill won the final and highest honour, the national entrepreneur of the year. I won the regional one. I was so happy that Bill liked COLD-FX. He is one of most admired entrepreneurs in Canada. Having his endorsement meant a lot to me.

Thinking back, I realize that, like Bill Comrie, many of our investors loved the product first. When the company and the board were trying to set up or refresh the company's vision and mission, I always insisted in putting "satisfactory to our consumers" first, even before shareholder's benefit— not always an easy argument to make for a public company. I firmly believed in the "word of mouth" grassroots marketing strategy, especially in the early days when the company had what I believed to be an unbeatable product, but with little money for general business operations, let alone for traditional advertising. In those early days, when we wanted to expand our market to eastern and central Canada and knowing we had little chance to raise money from institutional fund managers, I still went to Bay Street, building by building, pitching the company's business case. I personally convinced the money managers and stockbrokers to take our products and try them. At the end, few of them invested. However, the word from Bay Street, building by building? People were using COLD-FX! During election campaigns, one newspaper reported that politicians on Parliament Hill were passing COLD-FX around. I do not care too much about politicians, but I'm happy to know that COLD-FX kept them healthy and in good shape to debate with each other. It was all about raising awareness.

This was a time of many awards and honours. I was especially proud when I was viewed as a model for successful immigrants who had shared a similar journey to mine. In a 2005 award event in Toronto organized by the Chinese Business Chamber of Canada, I was showered with multiple awards: Best of Best of Chinese-Canadian Entrepreneur of the Year, Person of the Year in Chinese Business, The Most Improved Chinese Entrepreneur, and, a real favourite with me, The Favourite and Most Popular Young Female Business Person of the Year. The ethnic Chinese community were very proud of me being successful and recognized by "mainstream" Canadian markets.

Sales in Canada were so great that in early 2006, we made the bold but risky decision to move into the U.S. market. Many U.S. retailers had expressed strong interest and were impressed by our sales numbers in Canada. We met with a vice-president of pharmacy for Walmart in the United States who thought COLD-FX had a big future in the United States. With high hopes, we invested millions in our bid to capture our share of the American cold and flu market. But there was one problem: under FDA rules, we couldn't label the product as we could in Canada. In Canada, we could say COLD-FX was for colds and flu but in the United States, despite our success in the Phase 2 clinical trials, we were only allowed to say "may strengthen the immune system." We could not even refer to colds or flu on the bottle. (The news wasn't all bad: in February of 2007, smack in the middle of cold season, we received permission from Health Canada to make even stronger health claims for COLD-FX, specifically that it could help "reduce the frequency, severity and duration of cold and flu symptoms by boosting the immune system.")

In September 2006, we shipped millions of dollars' worth of product to many U.S. pharmacies, including Walmart. We had an aggressive marketing campaign with significant displays in all stores right from the beginning. That was amazing, as many brands could sell for years and not get the opportunity to sell full endcap product displays.

Initial retailer response was very positive. The launch quickly became a national effort, involving all major retailers, and we had secured close to 20,000 locations of distribution, including CVS and Walgreens. Strong initial shipments to new U.S. customers led to sales expectations that were much greater than the original forecasts.

Then the trouble began.

One of the big issues was how we reported revenues in our financial statements. On the advice of our accountants at the time, we based our revenue numbers on the money we were paid by retailers when they bought our product, which is called "sell-in," and referred to merchandise that was sold, invoiced, and delivered to the retailer. This figure, however, does not describe how much product the retailers sell to their customers, which is called "point of sale" (POS). That distinction didn't matter very much in Canada because retailers quickly sold the COLD-FX product that they bought from us. But in the United States, the landscape, as we would soon discover, was very different.

By the winter of 2007, storm clouds were building in the United States. COLD-FX was not selling as well as we had hoped there. In fact, several U.S. customers were returning a significant portion of their product. We were still hopeful, though, as our Canadian success had not happened overnight and it had taken time to build sales in Canada; it could be the same story in the United States.

That winter, we hired a new auditor. Now we were informed that we should use a different number to describe our revenues. The new national auditor told us that the "sell-in" to U.S. customers should be categorized as "customer deposits" and not as revenue. This was because the U.S. stores could return the product and ask for their money back if they could not sell it to consumers. This change did not affect our Canadian revenues, but it had a big impact on our U.S. results. It meant we had overestimated our sales revenue in the first quarter by $2.93 million.

The issue came to a head on April 11, 2007, when the board decided voluntarily to restate our previously released financial reports for the period from October to December, 2006. The decision sparked a firestorm. A week after the board meeting, the Alberta Security Commission (ASC) issued a temporary cease-trading order. Trading wasn't resumed until July 11, after we restated our financial reports.

It was a full-blown crisis, with sky-high costs for meetings with our accountants, lawyers, auditors, and business advisers that sometimes lasted to midnight. I had always worried about my "blind spot"—you do not know what you do not know, and that was my "blind spot" moment, when my worst nightmare became real. I dreamed about the crisis at night and woke up sweating.

I learned a valuable lesson during that painful time: always be very cautious when expanding to new markets— even if the retailers are enthusiastic and supportive. In hindsight, we should have hired more experienced operators, accountants, and lawyers before we expanded to a foreign market, but the reality was that we had taken a risk, it had not worked, and our stock price dropped. Our ambitious U.S. venture cost us dearly. By the end of our 2007 fiscal year, our U.S. sales were only a little over $1 million. Although our sales in Canada remained strong at $41 million, we lost $5.11 million before tax for the year.

Then came more ominous news: we were being investigated by the ASC on the grounds that in misstating our expected revenues, we had breached security law and acted contrary to the public interest.

Two years later, in 2009, came the well-publicized settlement. Of course, as CEO, I was one of the people named in the document. It is painful to read, even now. The ASC conducted an investigation, it wrote, into allegations "that Afexa Life Sciences (formerly CV Technologies) [had] breached the Alberta securities laws regarding continuous disclosure and acted contrary to the public interest."

After two years of exhausting, stressful crisis managing, we went for a settlement. The board agreed with the commission's findings—that in the first quarter of 2007 we had misstated our revenues based on sell-in to and stocking by retail, and on the historically low rate of product return in Canada. Although the regulator commended us for cooperating, and acknowledged our statement that we had intended no deceit, I was barred from being a director or executive officer of any public company for five years. We were fined $400,000, and I was personally fined $100,000 plus costs.

It was a crushing low point for me. I resigned most of my executive positions in the company (which in 2009 had been rebranded as Afexa Life Sciences) except for that of chief scientific officer. Someone had to take the fall. It should be and would be me because I was the CEO. I, along with my management team, simply had not had enough reporting experience when it came to expanding into the U.S. market, and the board and the settlement demanded a CEO who did have that experience. The management of the company I had co-founded had to be completely rejigged.

Our financial restatement due to the American mis-adventure also resulted in two coordinated shareholder class-action suits, which we settled for $7.1 million in 2010, while in no way admitting fault. The settlement was funded through our insurance coverage. It was simply the prudent thing to do for the business.

These were very tough times for the company and a period of self-doubt hell for me. During this time, my father was terminally ill back in China. He had been diagnosed with esophageal cancer and his lung cancer had come back after his remission six years ago. He had the second major surgery to remove the cancer in both his esophagus and lung in May 2007, but he would never get up again.

In the middle of managing the business crisis, and dawn-to-dusk meetings with lawyers and security inves-tigators, several times in a stretch of ten months I had to delay and reschedule meetings so that I could go back to China to be with my dying father. Dad passed away in our hometown, Jiujiang, at the age of seventy-four, on April 8, 2008, surrounded by his family, including me. A profound sadness and loss engulfed me during these days as I stayed by Dad's deathbed. Later on, I found extreme comfort in the decision I had made to be there with him in his last moments even though the business crisis back in Canada was reaching peaking. Watching Dad suffering from the illness, seeing his frail and tortured body attached to numerous tubes and ventilation machines, meeting his helpless eyes, seeing him wanting but not able to say his last words—for the first time as an adult, my whole life with my parents and my family was playing out again and again in front of my eyes, in my mind, and in my heart. I could not close my eyes for three days, and to clear my head I would go for intense runs around the lake in Jiujiang. I realized how much I loved my dad and how much he had given me by instilling in me a vulnerable yet strong character and spirit, all without saying much to me but this: keep your head down, work hard, and be honest. He told me not to value material things but to focus on my education and work hard. He told me philosophically, money was something never to take seriously, it does not come with your birth, you will not take it with you when you die. Heaven does not need money. Now I knew I had done what Dad wanted. I had wanted him to be proud of me and I knew he was very proud of me. I had used my knowledge and skill to develop what I believed were the best medicines for people's health. Along the way, to accomplish that, I had learned how to be a business leader, an unconventional one who would not feel that money is the ultimate success in life and in business. I had never done or intended to do anything for personal financial gain. But as a business leader in a public company, even with this kind of good intention, these beliefs were just not enough.

In the middle of grieving Dad's death, I also relieved myself of a tremendous load—guilt and self-doubt about my own business crisis back in Canada. I told myself I would be strong no matter what. "This shall pass, tomorrow is another day." I was ready to take any personal fall. However, deep in my heart, I knew that even if my wings were clipped, I would land on my feet; even if my knees were broken, I would still have arms and hands.

I had entered the business world as an ambitious young scientist with a burning desire to create a new paradigm of herbal medicines focusing on prevention and had to learn everything about running a business—how to manage people, how to raise money, how to lead a public company, how to satisfy consumers and shareholders. With no MBA and a quiet disposition that wasn't initially suited to Head Honcho-land, I had navigated a steep learning curve. But navigate it I did and I had finally arrived. I had always been confident in my science, but throughout the building of my company, I also felt proud of my ability to inspire investors, customers, and consumers, proud of my joy and skill in talking passionately about my products and its science. I could talk to fellow scientists, pharmacists, doctors, investors, and consumers and leave them believing in natural health products. I had been very lucky—I was invited on talk shows back at the very beginning, so I was forced to quickly improve my English-language presentation skills. (I also watched a lot of sitcoms to improve both my English and my understanding of the culture.) Meeting a wide range of people, such as hockey stars, premiers, the prime minister, and former U.S. president Bill Clinton had given me confidence.

These were very successful leaders whose own setbacks had been well publicized. But they were leaders. And in a much smaller sphere, I had become a leader too.

Much of my business learning had taken place in an enormously stressful environment. This stress affected me as a scientist; as a wife, mother, and daughter; and as an entrepreneur/executive who put everything she had on the line—after all, investors would expect nothing less from me. And I confess, it was hard not to take it personally when everything didn't play out to perfection.

In the three years after our American venture and our settlement with the ASC, the company was in constant restructuring (firing and hiring), crisis-managing mode—a revolving door of business advisers and professional managers who were in and out again. There was a changing of the guard. I was no longer a CEO and no longer on the board, but still a co-founder and chief scientific officer.

Stepping aside as CEO in 2009 and focusing on science again, I had gained some peace, leading research and product development in discovering more formulations for future product pipelines, working with our clinical team to do more clinical tests, and travelling and working with our scientific advisers and clinical collaborators to advance our science. Scarlett O'Hara may have had Tara, but thank God, I always had science to fall back on. Those three years were actually among the most creative and productive years I had as a chief scientist.

Our research in the lab and clinical trials led to the discovery of new formulations for the treatment of diabetes, high cholesterol, hypertension, herpes, and cancer.

In collaboration with Dr. Ken Rosenthal at McMaster University, we would also discover new phytochemicals that could activate the natural receptors (toll-like-receptors) in immune cells. It was a scientific discovery that found the ultimate piece in a very complicated mechanism involving the action of natural compounds on the immune system. These phytochemicals, called TLR agonists (toll-like receptor regulators), showed positive results in killing H1N1 (a flu virus) and HSV-1 and HSV-2 (both herpes viruses) in laboratory studies in Dr. Rosenthal's lab. We filed patents for this.

During this time, we also collaborated with Dr. Sandra Miller, a professor and immunologist at McGill University. We tested CVT-E002, the active ingredients in COLD-FX, on cancer mice in her lab. The results were marvellous. Dr. Miller was thrilled that all her sick mice had survived after taking CVT-E002. What's more, the mice that had ingested CVT-E002 had an increased level of immune cells known as natural killer cells. We filed several patents for these discoveries.

We travelled to Wake Forest University in Winston-Salem, North Carolina, to work with the doctors and researchers in its Cancer Research Center and to discuss a clinical study on cancer patients. The National Cancer Institute — the most important cancer research body in the world — then sponsored this landmark trial of CVT-E002 to protect chronic lymphocytic leukemia patients from colds and flu. This trial showed positive results for CVT-E002 reducing the symptoms in moderate to severe acute respiratory infection. The results were presented at the annual meeting of American Society of Clinical Oncology in Chicago in 2010.

We worked out another formulation with extracts from two medicinal herbs (not ginseng) and discovered it had a remarkable effect in lowering bad cholesterol and raising good cholesterol in animals. Working with a group of clinicians from UCLA in Los Angeles and the University of Alberta, we showed promising results from this formulation in humans as well. So we filed for a patent for this discovery.

By the last quarter of 2011, we had dramatically increased our patent portfolio, with more than 230 issued or pending, including 61 patents issued globally with 13 patent families. By that time, we had completed 26 clinical trials, with two more trials ongoing and five in the planning stages. We had published in more than twenty peer-reviewed publications and had presented our findings in forty conferences.

I was back to being a determined, focused chief scientist. Of course, this time around, I had a bigger team and more experience in managing science than when I first started. We had a team of close to fifty people working in product development, clinical research, and manufacturing support and quality control. The team included twenty-one Ph.D.s and nine M.Sc.s with expertise in chemistry, biology, pharmacology, immunology, cardiovascular, neurology, process engineering, and quality development. Using a collaborative model with university researchers also allowed these studies to be time- and cost-effective. I was pleased with these results and was strategizing and working on a five-year plan of developing and launching these products.

In spite of this activity, the company started losing money and showing more and more of a disconnect between science and marketing, even though the sales of COLD-FX were still relatively strong and it remained the top cold and flu brand in Canada. With the increasing cost of running the business, the company was barely breaking even. The headlines were negative. I knew it wouldn't be long before we once again had to address the question of our very survival. And, sadly, I wasn't wrong.

In the last quarter of 2011, after fending off a hostile takeover from another large company, Afexa Life Sciences was sold to Valeant Pharmaceuticals International Inc., one of Canada's largest drug makers. The press release Valeant issued was sunny: "We are pleased to have the full support of Afexa's management team and board of directors for a transaction that we believe should deliver significant benefits to our customers, employees and shareholders," Valeant chairman and chief executive officer J. Michael Pearson said in a statement. "Afexa's product line, combined with our portfolio ... will provide the critical mass we need in the [over-the-counter] market and should provide Valeant Canada with another platform for growth."

But I felt anything but sunny. The price — $89 million — was fair to shareholders compared to its then stock price in the market. (As I was by then a minority shareholder, I got only a fraction of this.) And it was comforting to know that shareholders and investors who had stuck with us through the hard times still got a good return.

Nonetheless, I felt incredibly sad. You would think I would be proud that something I had created and built from scratch, something I had nurtured, had tremendous value. By that time, of course, I was not at all the sole proprietor. I was a co-founder, but a minority shareholder in a biotech company after many years of diluting through share issuing.

However, I felt the company was my baby, the one I gave birth to and nurtured to maturity. I was still focused on the new formulations and new findings. We were working on making a five-year business plan. To me, the journey was not over, and I had real hope that the company would turn around and return to double-digit growth like before. How could I possibly let go?

Anyone who has had to surrender his or her company knows the drill: you get acquired, you sign, and the new team moves in. The only thing absent, from your point of view, is the insane protective love you feel for this enterprise that the new people can't possibly know or feel.

The acquisition process lasted a few months before it all ended for me and most of my staff in Edmonton. During this time, more bad news and publicity: CBC's *Marketplace* was doing a story critical of COLD-FX. I became aware of this only because of an ambush interview by a reporter while I was walking to my car after giving a lecture in Fort Edmonton Park. This was the first—and I hope it's the last—time this type of interview ever happened to me. Inside, I was not too panicked because I had nothing to hide. But I was annoyed with this type of antic from a reputable network. I kept smiling while I told the interviewer that the company had been sold and I was no longer the spokesperson. I already had a heavy heart, having sold the company. Now the flagship product itself was being attacked as ineffective, and I did not think I could handle any more bad news. In a way, it was a relief that I was no longer responsible for managing and answering these questions. When the show was aired, I refused to watch it. It obviously raised doubts about COLD-FX's quality, efficacy, and the science behind it.

I realize now that I was being too discreet with the reporter, saying quietly I couldn't talk about it. While it was legally correct that I no longer owned the company or the product, I could have still, as a proud co-inventor, scientist, and consumer, pointed out how well COLD-FX worked and how many thousands and thousands of people it had helped. Would that have changed their minds? Nope. You can never win a media war.

Through all of this, I never doubted my worth as a scientist or as a natural health pioneer. As a scientist, I've only ever talked about facts and what I know. The problem, from my point of view, was that some people did not understand the science or misinterpreted the science. In general, people have a hard time with something that's new. It's seen as just too risky. And here is a truth that doesn't need a clinical trial to back it up: we scientists do not always know how to sell ourselves. We don't do a good job of explaining. It doesn't come as naturally as our sheer stubborn doggedness in the lab.

Privately, though, I felt embarrassed. Were people talking about me? Asking themselves what Jackie was going to do now? As a scientist, I had failed many times—you can't be doing experiments and not fail. But I had never failed publicly before. What were they whispering?

Letting go was hard for other reasons. I felt a tremendous responsibility toward my staff. All the people we had brought together had worked with us for many, many years and showed a great loyalty. I worried about them. And that's how it should be. Whatever your private sadness or executive worries, employees depend on you for their livelihood. It's only right to feel responsible.

When the company made the deal to sell, we believed the new owners would not only continue to develop the brand and the science behind it but also develop the large product pipeline that was still in development, which included products for diabetes, high cholesterol, hypertension, even cancer. I should have known better and understood that Valeant had a different business model and vision to grow its business, not by developing but by acquiring and selling cash-generating products. But that day, when a whole troop of people came in from Valeant's acquisition team, I had a sharp stabbing realization we were not going to be continuing in any new creative venture, we were not going to be sticking around to continue our journey and business. It was over.

Many of our staff were in shock when they received their employment termination notice and final paycheque. I was in shock too. I behaved well, as a senior person, but it took me a couple of days to realize there was no point to linger or—how can I say this—give rein to my emotions. It was hard, it was wrenching. My scientific team felt badly for me, but I felt worse for them. There was little time to absorb my own shock. It was not a good time. My staff gave me a surprise party—it was emotional—and they made a very nice album for me with lots of pictures, lots of good wishes, which I found very moving. "You have inspired me with your passion, intelligence and humble character. An individual with your character will always succeed in everything you do" was one heartfelt message that brought tears to my eyes. Another staff member praised our company culture: "Everyone is so kind and generous and passionate ... a great company." The staff gave me—what else?—a statue of a phoenix rising. (Later I called my new company Afinix after that phoenix and its message of regeneration. But I still had a few more months of transition trauma to get through.)

All that time, I was still working like mad trying to spin off a company with the patents and research on a product pipeline outside of COLD-FX. In a goodwill gesture, Valeant gave me (with a few senior executive and managers) two months to find money for a spinoff so I could take over the employment of the scientific team. It was hard not to panic—we were working madly to come up a three-year plan; so far, it was showing that we needed $20 to $30 million to operate.

For a frenetic two months, I pitched. People still believed in me—especially some longtime COLD-FX investors and colleagues. I was also so much more experienced than when I first set out to pitch those many years ago. I talked to some venture investors in Hong Kong, I talked to my friends. The deadline for firming the deals up was looming. If I couldn't come up with the money to register a spinoff and get it up and running by the end of December, I would have to close my doors. I tried—I knocked on so many doors, government, business. But the hard reality was it had taken me more than ten years to establish my company and you can't redo it in two months. There was no way to find that kind of money in such a short time.

I had to accept that it was not possible to spin off such a company. So in December 2011, I had to leave the company. I no longer held any shares or position. I sat in my half-packed office and felt like crying. On December 23, 2011, for the last time, I left the COLD-FX building in Edmonton Research Park, a proud landmark that we built for $12 million from the ground up when we were profitable in the years from 2005 to 2007. In this building, I had opened up our lab to local elementary schools for their science trips. Today it sits empty. I believe it now belongs to the City of Edmonton. For several years, every time I drove by the empty parking lot, my memories would flood back. But I'm feeling that sharp pain less and less these days.

After almost two decades, the COLD-FX journey had come to an end for me. All that effort, all that research, all that time. An iconic product—my baby—was no longer mine to be proud of.

Most of the staff had been given notice by then. There was not a lot of time to focus on my own problems—many others were in a worse position than I was. We had hired many young graduates in the last few years. One was halfway through a government internship as part of her post-Ph.D. training and there was no way I could fail her. So I hired her, and the funding agency allowed her to move her remaining six-month scholarship and continue her internship with me. She did not disappoint me—she did a great job in eventually helping me set up a new company, including business planning.

Right after the sale, I started living and planning my life on a smaller scale—not at all corporate. I had gone from 120 employees to three, and that small group would meet every week in the golf club coffee shop. I went to those meetings wearing what I called my Sunday clothes—comfortable flats and sweaters. I had never drunk coffee in my life, but I started drinking coffee then as we batted around ideas. I was back to the beginning.

Still, after the initial shock and sadness had worn off, I had no regrets. Maybe we had been too premature going into the United States. But given the opportunity, I would certainly go back to the States again and try to sell my product. Who wouldn't want a globally successful health product?

One thing had definitely changed—I no longer wanted to lead a public company. Many CEOs have told me the same thing. Sometimes public companies and true entrepreneurialism just don't mix.

On the other hand, I had never imagined we would be so successful in Canada. And if we hadn't made those mistakes, how could I get even stronger, how would I be able to develop more new products and make an even bigger impact next time? I already felt that phoenix rising.

This period was a time of deep thought for me, a time of feeling wounded and, at first, unsure about how to move forward. But you can't keep me down for long.

Both the success and the setbacks had a profound effect on how I would eventually reconstitute myself and on my goals in forming my new company.

With my family's relatively simple lifestyle, I had made enough money for us to be comfortable, for my children to be educated, for my husband and me to not worry about eventual retirement. But as I have said, money was never my chief goal.

Seeing my great success in Canada, my parents had been extremely proud of me, just as they were delighted with my sister and brother who have good jobs back in China.

But now my father was dead and my mother was puzzled. In China, if you don't have a job, you cannot survive. My mom said sadly to me, "You don't have a job anymore." I replied in what I hoped was a reassuring tone of voice, "I don't need one, we can survive." And really I didn't need a job, I needed a purpose. Faithful supporters like Don Cherry sent me nice notes, alluding to my drive. Some friends said, "Jackie, you will never let the grass grow under your feet."

Already thinking of how I was going to rebuild and refinance another company, I said to my husband, "Let's remortgage the house." He looked at me and said, "Why don't you just stay home?"

And so, for at least two weeks, I became a desperate housewife.

5.

# BRINGING IT HOME

Although I joke about becoming a "desperate housewife" after the company sold, it wasn't funny at the time. I hadn't expected the company would be sold. I was very disappointed in the outcome. I felt bruised and burned. In the last four years, I had gone through an excruciating time, and then most recently consoled myself by throwing myself into science and creativity. I admit it was a challenge for me at first to put it all into perspective. At times, I saw myself as a failure, even though, realistically, that didn't make sense: I had started a company, created a successful brand, made tons of money for some investors. But instead of seeing the whole arc of my career, I was living in the present tense. I moped around. I drove my husband crazy. Sure, it allowed me to spend more time with my sons, Nicholas, fifteen, and Alex, eleven, but even they thought Mom should be working. As my younger son said, "Mom, you can't stay home, you need to work, we need the money to survive!" We didn't—I had made enough to support my family after handing over all my shares to the purchaser of my company.

And Eugene, an engineer, had a good job. Besides, as I've said, we lead a very simple life. I didn't have tons of money but I had enough so that if I wanted to stay home and just be a wife and mom, I could.

At first I was as busy at home as I had been at work—organizing, seeing my household with fresh and alarmed eyes. My kids were still in bunk beds and they were too old for that! So I went house hunting and found us a better, bigger house. My boys finally had their own individual bedrooms, although they still had to share a bathroom.

Slowly I made peace with myself and started to look at things from a different perspective.

What I was facing as I neared fifty was no different from what many men and women my age were facing: a new chapter of my working life, a transition, a sense that I now had a chance, after two decades of nonstop gruelling scientific and business work in getting my company and COLD-FX off the ground, to make some different decisions about how I wanted to spend my time and my intellectual capital.

I was no longer that young scientist in my twenties, who took a chance on a huge adventure and began my own biotech company. Back then, work was my whole life. As long as I had clothes to keep me warm, food to fill my stomach, and a bed to sleep in, I was fine. My interest has always been research and the results of research.

You might say the life of the lab had created a very narrow focus for me. Of course I had my marriage, and everyday beauty in my life—music, a walk, a run. And the upside to this narrow focus was that I had a strong sense of self-worth as I spent my days going to the lab. I felt that what I was doing was important.

Looking back at the beginning, both my husband—a very good master graduate computer engineer who gave up many job offers in the 1990s to stay in Alberta with me—and I had been very career-driven. We did, however, establish an unspoken rule that when we were home together, we wouldn't talk about work. Home was a place for peace and quiet. I compartmentalized. We had known each other since we were hardworking students, and we had learned early how to put our work aside and just be together. There was music to listen to and, for me (I confess), sitcoms to watch. They made me laugh and continued to give me a better sense of the English language and North American culture.

In truth, I didn't have much interest in the outside world anyway—I was pretty occupied by what was in my brain, and life in the lab and office. Once I had been in the student bubble. I was still in the bubble, but it had become the entrepreneurial bubble. The difference between the two? The entrepreneurial bubble can burst at any moment—it's called running out of money and risking everything, including your reputation.

While I was initially building my business, we had waited to start a family. In fact, my husband, who saw me as focused and driven, was a little shocked in the late 1990s when I told him I thought we should now start having children. (Kind of like that marriage proposal I made to him—right out of the blue.) He said he wasn't even sure I wanted them! But I always had, even though I hadn't talked much about it.

I had my first child—son Nicholas—in 1998, at one of the most demanding times in the development of the company. But I knew if I didn't have a child then it would be too late. I didn't really even think about life and work and how to balance the two, because my instincts told me I would find a way. But I was also a little crazy at the time. I took almost no time off—I had someone get me a fax machine at my bedside the day after I gave birth.

How was I going to deal with a new baby while I pushed my company? I had a solution. I would ask my parents to come over from China to help us, and they agreed. They had never been to Canada before, their visa was late in coming, and they finally arrived about two weeks after I had given birth. Of course, by then I was already back working. My mom gave me hell. In Chinese tradition, during the first month after you give birth you are not supposed to lift a finger. The windows have to be sealed, and you are supposed to not touch anything while your bones and muscles heal from this great trauma of birth. They say the wind is not supposed to get in your bones. Now how could I do that, how could I never leave my bed? Impossible! So I just kept on doing what I did, and Mom kept on giving me grief. But really, they were a wonderful help.

Talking things over with my mom now that she lived with me, recalling my own childhood, I realized how guilty she felt about not spending much time with me when I was little, about how the demands of being a government worker during the stress-filled Cultural Revolution meant she had not been able to be there for me. In fact, she cried a lot when she told me this. I reassured her that I had turned

With Mom in downtown Calgary in fall 2012. Mom loves to see different places, and now and then, I travel with her. This was one of those trips.

out just fine, and that she has been a lovely mom to me. It makes me sad to say this, but I too, under very different circumstances, now feel guilty about not spending enough time with my own kids when they were very little. My life was the opposite of hers—I had moved to a country that gave me every freedom and opportunity. And I gratefully took advantage of those freedoms to pursue a high-risk but rewarding career. Did I put my business first? I'm not sure I can stand to put it that way, but I sure worked all the time. I think about it a lot these days—how did I end up replicating my own mother's role? Maybe it was just in my nature to work that hard.

In January 2012, looking for things to do, I agreed to be "the corporate walking chair" for the Leukemia and Lymphoma Society of Canada in Edmonton, a volunteer position. Working with the organization for nine months to help raise awareness and funds was a satisfying way to change the channel for me. I led the Light the Night Walk. I took my whole family (my sons reached the finish line first) and my three staff to the park. That night, it was announced that we had exceeded the fundraising target for that year. That alone gave me a tremendous sense of accomplishment and comfort that I could still do things and help others in a totally unconditional and giving way.

As my boys began to experience their adolescent years, I became far more involved as a parent, volunteering in their schools and monitoring their homework. I am no Tiger Mom, but sometimes they tell me I am mean because I criticize them for slacking off and insist they work harder.

When it comes to balance I work smarter now—mostly out of my home office. I encourage others on my small staff to do the same. I am not prepared to sacrifice my family to my new venture. This brings up another question that is a big part of any public conversation about science—how women carve out careers in science, what the obstacles are, and why there are these obstacles. A recent *New York Times* article said that North American women studying in the STEM disciplines—science, technology, engineering, and math—still face stereotyping and discrimination that can hold them back. But it noted that women in science who come from other cultures seem less affected by discrimination based on sex. In my case, that may well be true. When I grew up in China, there was one lucky thing when it came to gender. The politics of the Cultural Revolution were punishing, but they made no distinction between boys and girls in terms of work. So I never felt discriminated against because I was a girl. I was not always the smartest, but I just worked extremely hard and became very self-disciplined. My drive was innate in my character—I was always terrified of not knowing enough. But at the same time, if this isn't a contradiction, I gradually became very grounded in my science. I just did the work. The work itself made me very happy. I believe people don't talk enough about how much they love their work (if they're lucky)—and I have always loved mine. I also think pharmacology and physiology are more accepting of women and the lives they want to lead. An academic life is pretty compatible with family life. Business can be more so, if you set it up that way. It's usually more demanding and involves risk-taking, but the upside is that if you're the boss, you at least get to allocate your own time.

In some ways, I have an old-fashioned view of being a woman. I never wanted to be masculine in any way. I was not aggressive, I was not even very political or strategic in the way I did things. I would just ask for things very directly and go with my intuitional common sense.

I do think women are different from men—we want different things. We measure ourselves by work, but also very much by the success of our home lives. Are our marriages happy? Our kids thriving? If not, we take that personally, we assume responsibility.

I know I do. Nothing can make me feel guiltier than feeling that I let my kids down in any way.

But we are no different from men when it comes to going for success and satisfaction in our work. Right from the start I was lucky to have had an amazing mentor in Peter Pang, who very much believed in me, encouraging me to take more responsibility and not to be afraid to make mistakes. When I first arrived in Canada, that was so helpful to me— it gave me confidence. This is the role I want to play with young graduate students and aspiring professors and managers today. I want to say to them, you can do what you want and I will show you how.

I was aware many times, especially in those early years, that in business, because I was a woman, small and quiet, people could easily dismiss me. They could deliberately not notice me in the room or even around the board table. But I had my own way of doing things, and once people who worked with me realized how determined I was, how stubborn, how I would never—ever—give up, I think I earned their respect.

I'm proud of the leadership skills I developed, but I developed them the hard way—first in the lab through leading, at Dr. Pang's suggestion, several big research teams. And then through starting my own company and learning how to talk about science to investors, how to sit on boards, how to get my point across in the way that makes them listen. I still would say I do not like to argue and debate, but I certainly like to passionately talk about what I've discovered and what I know. The process and the product are things I can talk endlessly about. I think a lot of it is that I have a tremendous sense of responsibility. If I don't tell people how wonderful my product is, then why should anyone else? I have been passionately trying to get people to invest in my ideas and my business for years. When you're looking for necessary financing, shyness disappears pretty fast. One year, on Bay Street, I was hustled from office to office, only twenty minutes a meeting, forcefully making my pitch, until I finally told the people who were setting up these meetings, slow down! You're not walking in high heels! And don't fault me for the heels—I am 5 foot 2 and I needed them for effect. But I enjoyed making the pitch, connecting with potential investors.

I also think that being a woman helps me deal with consumers, the public—I am approachable and down to earth, and people have said, "Jackie, I trust your science, I trust what you have to say on this."

As for work-life balance, I've never been very good at it, as you might have gathered. I've always been focused on a goal. I still find it hard, as the leader of a company, to carve out personal time for myself. But I'm trying. I sought out old friends not too long ago, and for my fiftieth birthday, I met one of my oldest student friends from China in Paris. It was a fantastic reunion, not only strolling around that amazing city but talking intently about our lives since we had studied together in Shanghai. My friend had left science for interior design. We talked about our work, our lives, about our kids, our husbands. I found it so reassuring to be back in touch. Recently, on a visit to Niagara Falls, I met a whole group of classmates from my student days in Shanghai and again, we all couldn't stop talking. It was funny—I found myself becoming that girl again, a bit shy, one of the youngest of the bunch. Many of them were very accomplished in work and in life, but so was I. And there I was, taking on more risk, starting another company. Lots to reflect on.

Another trip that meant so much to me personally was our family trip to China. I wanted the boys to see where their parents had studied—right near Tiananmen Square. I wanted them to see the country that had given us both our starts. Our education at the time had been mostly free—it isn't any more—but that's something I have always been extremely grateful for. My family had not at all been financially equipped to send me on to higher education. Without tuition being free, I would never have ended up at the Shanghai First Medical School and later the Chinese Academy of Medical Sciences, where I got an excellent education and training.

We first-generation strivers from China who found our way to North America all seem to have much in common—pride in our education, and in the wealth of knowledge we have brought to our new country. But also, we have the same watchful attitude toward our children, living a much more comfortable life. We worry they are too safe, too comfortable. We don't want ambition bred out of our children. We want them to strive as hard as we did.

My girlfriends and I also talked about our physical changes. After the company was acquired by Valeant, I had a profound physical experience that helped me focus on what I wanted to do next. Menopause—perimenopause—was very difficult for me both emotionally and physically. At one time, I thought I was depressed, my moods were so uneven. My joints ached, my belly was bloating, I was so very tired and worn down. Some of it might have been an abrupt let-down from the brutal pace at which I had been going for years. But some of it was clearly age-related. How could I make myself feel better naturally? What natural health products could restore vitality and a sense of vibrancy to my life and to the lives of other busy, career-driven women like me?

I began thinking about all these things, going for long hikes in the beautiful Edmonton River Valley with my girlfriends—and with my very fit mom—trying to get a handle on what I wanted to do next. They say during a transition that you have to acknowledge that something has ended; you have to let something go before you can take on something new. I now had the sense that something had to change. And that something was me.

# 6.

# STARTING OVER

We formed and registered a new company, Afinix Life Sciences Inc., on January 21, 2012. I had been home only a few weeks after leaving Valeant before I took the plunge. I remember thinking, *Well, here I go again*. Afinix was a play on the word "phoenix" as well as a continuation of the "A" words I like so much. Later we changed the company name to reflect the brand name of our products—Afinity Life Sciences.

Why did I do it? Why did I want to create another natural health product company? First of all, it was my response to my sense of a setback. It was my way to cope. It was a way to feel better. I would continue doing what I love to do, what I do best. It meant taking on financial risk again—most consumer-oriented ventures have a 50-50 chance of succeeding. My goal was to create and build a life science brand that Canadians would trust and turn to first when it comes to natural health products.

But remembering the 100 or so employees who had lost their jobs when Valeant acquired us and let them go, I think founding a new company was also my way of creating hope. Isn't that what entrepreneurs do best? They point to a future.

I had two main thoughts in my mind. One was that because the previous company—and my flagship product—had been sold, I could no longer identify myself as being the person who built that. For years, every time I got on a plane and someone asked me what I did, I told them about COLD-FX, and they would be impressed. Who was I now? But I did change how I thought about that history, that accomplishment, and know it is mine forever.

I also felt strongly I should continue to do what I wanted to do; I still felt expectations coming from people cheering me on and supporting me—that phoenix rising thing. *I need to do this*, I thought. *I need to show everyone I have another chapter in me, that I am not a failure.*

People who know me wonder how my successes—creating the number-one brand in cold and flu consumer products in Canada, and selling the company for $89 million—could ever make me feel badly about myself. I suppose I am hard on myself. Before the company had been acquired by Valeant, I had gone through one of the lowest points in my life. In the aftermath, I found myself thinking again and again, *If only the company had been run better* … I took it so personally. I wasn't thinking about the whole twenty-five years, about how much we had actually accomplished. But now in more recent years I have become very proud again of all that we did.

I knew I could not continue what I'd been doing—COLD-FX along with all the patents and product pipeline belonged to the new owner now. I needed to develop different new products.

In 2012, when I was approaching fifty, I took a look at the market made up of people like me. All the research shows a huge aging baby boomer cohort with high hopes and every expectation that they will age better than their parents.

Between 2006 and 2011, the number of Canadians over the age of sixty-five increased from 13% of the population to over 14% of the total population, and it's not going to stop growing. It's called the "aging tsunami." This age group is expected to be the fastest-growing segment of the Canadian population over the next twenty-five years and is projected to become more numerous than young children in Canada by 2017.

We in this post–forty-five cohort will be recognized as the most affluent-growing segment of the population, one that requires a lot of servicing, with an ever-changing list of specific health-care products and services. And not just in the so-called medical mainstream.

Today's active agers like me are searching for natural health treatments, for both maintaining and improving general health, and in managing age-related specific health issues and their treatments, such as high cholesterol, cognition changes, arthritis pain, lack of energy and increasing fatigue, and symptoms related to menopause and andropause.

I believe that Canada's aging population is one of the key factors driving the demand for vitamins, supplements, and natural health products in Canada. As the aging trend continues, marketers of vitamins and natural health products have been adapting to this change by focusing on the needs of older consumers.

Much of the relatively affluent market, as I have said, is made up of highly self-aware men and women who are interested in their well-being on every possible level—emotional, financial, environmental, and social. Boomers grew into adulthood thinking about themselves in a different way than the previous generation did—a little less humbly. Think of L'Oreal's brilliant hair product line "I'm worth it." Rightly or wrongly, that is the ethos of a generation.

But in order to enjoy all that you're worth, you have to be as healthy as you can. People today are living well into their nineties, and there are now accepted truths about those who are the happiest and getting the most out of their senior years. They are the ones who stay physically active and remain socially connected. They take care of themselves, often turning to natural health products to do so.

Right from the start of my new venture, I decided that we should develop natural health products for this aging population. We wouldn't restrict ourselves to the immune system, as we did with COLD-FX. Instead we would address many concerns of the body as we age—our hearts, brains, joints, skin, and energy.

This time, I would take a different innovative approach. Since we could not afford to do clinical trials at the beginning, we would take a very well studied and approved class of natural ingredient, use the best technology to make it the purest and most potent, and formulate it into health condition–specific products.

I knew what natural health product I wanted to produce from the very start. It is a very pure, highly potent form of omega-3 fatty acids.

I have always been fascinated by omega-3s. They're a group of non-saturated fatty acids that exist in nature and in human bodies. Non-saturated essential fatty acids are, as they sound, fats that are necessary within the human body. Without them, you could cause serious damage to different systems within the body. Naturally you should also go to the source by eating fish once or twice a week. But even the Mayo Clinic says, "People who have heart disease may benefit from supplements of omega-3 fatty acids and should discuss this with their doctors."

So what can omega-3s do for active agers? Just about everything good. They can reduce inflammation, sharpen the mind, and improve the cardiovascular system. They can help our organs to function properly and help cell walls to form. They can help to circulate oxygen through our bodies. They have been shown to improve learning, memory, and mood, and reduce anxiety and depression. They have also been shown to reduce age-related cognitive decline and help to maintain eye health and proper vision.

They can even improve the body's immune response. Omega-3s act to reduce the amount of arachidonic acid in immune cells, thereby reducing their inflammatory response. This feature is important because inflammation is involved in so many allergic conditions and chronic diseases. Reducing inflammation has other benefits, such as the maintenance of proper skin health, improved joint and gut function, and a reduction in biologic aging.

Some studies show that omega-3s stop DNA segments called telomeres from shortening, a key to having a long, healthy life. The longer your telomeres, the less vulnerable your cells are to becoming weak and damaged.

So the potential of omega-3s to help active agers is extraordinary. Take arthritis. It's one of the most common health issues among aging populations. According to Statistics Canada, in 2011 there were 4.75 million Canadians—16% of the population—who suffered from arthritis. Broken down by gender, the group was 63% female and 37% male. The number of Canadians suffering from arthritis by 2031 will increase to 7 million, which would represent about 20% of the population. The more than 100 different forms of arthritis include osteoarthritis, rheumatoid arthritis, fibromyalgia, and gout. The disease is the leading cause of disability in Canada, and the burden on the Canadian economy has been estimated at more than $33 billion annually.

Cardiovascular disease (CVD) is another common health problem among aging adults. As reported by Health Canada in 2005, CVD represented 11.6% of the total Canadian cost of illness classifiable by diagnostic category. Statistics Canada found that between 2007 and 2009, CVD became a huge burden on our health-care system.

How do omega-3 fatty acids work to support cardiovascular health? Numerous studies indicate that omega-3 fatty acids reduce several risk factors for cardiovascular diseases by decreasing blood triglyceride levels, reducing resting heart rate, controlling heart rhythm, and decreasing vascular inflammation, blood clotting, and blood pressure.

Omega-3 fatty acids can help to keep aging brains healthy too. Cognitive impairment, including Alzheimer disease and other types of dementia, can be a big challenge for people as they age. A report from the Alzheimer Society of Canada indicates that these conditions affect one in four Canadians over the age of 65 and will increase to two out of three Canadians over the age of 85. With our aging population, the number of cases of cognitive impairment is expected to double in Canada over the next 30 years, reaching epidemic levels.

How do omega-3 fatty acids help? These fatty acids, in particular one known as DHA, are one of the major structural components of brain cells, making up approximately 60% of the total polyunsaturated fatty acids in the neuronal membranes. So they significantly influence a number of membrane-related functions that affect the memory and learning abilities. Several studies have indicated that omega-3 fatty acids can improve age-related cognitive decline in the elderly.

So all in all, omega-3s have tremendous potential to help active agers be healthier. But when we checked the market, the quality of the products was inconsistent. At first, we did a simple market study by looking into the labels of more than two dozen omega-3 based products. The purity, potency, and functional claims are all over the place on these labels. We then set out to do some hard-core studies by testing some well-known and leading brands for purity, potency, and their anti-inflammatory–like effects in cultured human cells. These tests were done in reputable third-party labs, including the National Institute for Nanotechnologies under the National Research Council.

The results surprised even us. We looked at the purity of two of the key omega-3 fatty acids—DHA and EPA, polyunsaturated fatty acid. The purity ranged from very low (20%) up to 65%. I figured we could do better than that. Our Afinity brand was about 70% pure. Being a pharmacologist, I care more about the impurity part—what's in the portion of a capsule other than its active omega-3s? Does it contain natural chemicals, environmental pollutants, and contaminants or something else? Do these impurities create a health hazard? Do they interfere with the active ingredients and suppress the desirable anti-inflammatory effect of EPA and DHA?

The test results were revealing. Some products had low levels of the good fatty acids but contained excessive amounts of the bad saturated fatty acids. Worse, some products even contained trans fats. This suggests the extraction or purification process of that particular product was poorly controlled. Some products also contained excessive oxidative chemicals, resulting again from a poorly designed or poorly controlled manufacturing process or storage conditions that exposed the product to too much oxidation.

Here, then, was our opportunity. Omega-3 products are already an established natural health product category, one of biggest and fastest-growing market categories in the natural health industry. We could enter an established market like this quickly.

And we could deliver what active agers truly needed—a reliable and pure supply of omega-3s. We had an edge in the experience and expertise we had accumulated in the last twenty-five years as we developed natural health products, including COLD-FX. We had a superior technology and science that assures consumers of the quality, potency, and purity of our product. We would set out to be the best in a very crowded market. I would not put my name behind our brand if I did not believe we could provide consumers with a high-quality product that offers great value and assistance with their health.

So began my new company, Afinity. I spent the first twelve months with five other trusted colleagues and friends planning the business and design technology and products. We threw in our own money and worked for free. We had one paid employee, a young Ph.D. graduate intern. We successfully applied for a few small grants to help us test our scientific ideas. At the end of the first year, we had already created three formulations in the areas of women's health, men's health, and mental and physical fatigue. In addition, we identified a unique proprietary technology that can produce highly potent and pure omega-3 fish oils. Following initial tests, results came out showing the superior quality and efficacy of this active omega-3 ingredient.

I started taking the product myself and felt notable differences. My nails were stronger, my hair looked healthier, and my skin glowed. My mood was better and I wasn't so fatigued. I was motivated again to go to the gym regularly, so my belly fat disappeared. I came back from my physical low and thought that after all, there is a light at the end of the tunnel.

I was excited again and felt there was a tremendous potential in developing this product to become the top brand in this growing category of omega-3 fish oil. Again, we worked day and night on perfecting the product formulation and quality specification. We submitted four condition-specific omega-3-based products to Health Canada for approval. They were all approved in a few months.

In the second year, we put more of our own money into the venture and worked very hard to apply for other sources of funding needed for product development and business activities. We were able to hire more staff, bringing our employee count up to eight.

We decided to do a soft product launch, selling our product online and using social media to build excitement and generate awareness, followed by a more public launch in September of 2013 when we felt ready to support our approach to retailers. We successfully applied for an additional $1.5 million investment from AVAC Ltd. on the condition we invested at least $1.5 million of our own. AVAC is the private Alberta-based investment company that had helped us in the early commercial stages of building the COLD-FX brand.

We are totally focused on the purity of our product. As just about everyone knows, the best source of omega-3 EPAs and DHAs are from fish oil, but it all depends on which fish you use. Smaller is better—fish like anchovies and sardines, which aren't on any endangered species list. We searched around the world to select the manufacturer who could best use the cutting-edge purification technology to deliver the

With my younger son, Alex, 10, at the launching event of Afinity Brand on
September 11, 2013. I was very proud that Alex presented himself so well
and helped sell the first batch of Afinity products.

product that met our technical and purity standards. We also identified the very best and most sustainable fish source to get our Afinity omega-3s.

Ensuring that the product is pure is a challenge. Omega-3 products should be molecularly distilled in a low-temperature setting to remove impurities and avoid generating trans fats and oxidative chemicals. Saturated fatty acids often come with impurities such as trans fats; oxidation chemicals such as hydroperoxides; environmental pollutants and contaminants accumulated in fish oil such as toxic chemicals like PCBs, dioxins, and furans; heavy metals like mercury, arsenic, cadmium, and lead; pesticides; and microbial contaminants (bacteria, yeast, and mould).

There should also be antioxidants like vitamin E in the mix, which help to extend the quality, freshness, and shelf life of fish-oil products.

To create a pure and reliable product, we are relying on labs that possess leading-edge technology, analytical equipment, and most of all, first-class scientific research experts. We are very fortunate that because of our in-depth knowledge and experience in natural product research, we have an extensive research network that I have been able to collaborate with over the last twenty-five years.

We are confident about the purity of our Afinity omega-3 product. Working with testing labs, we set up a panel of more than twenty test parameters to evaluate the purity standards. The majority of these parameters are devoted to meet the purity standards set by Health Canada and international institutes like the Council for Responsible Nutrition, the Global Organization for EPA and DHA Omega-3, and the International Fish Oil Standards Program.

Based on these testing results, we know that the purity of the top-selling omega-3 supplements usually ranges from 20% to 60% pure, with the average about 35%. Contrast that with prescription omega-3 products that are 85% to almost 90% pure. This finding confirmed for me that there was more than enough room to create and market an omega-3 natural health product that comes from proprietary, cutting-edge purification technology and that comes in at more than 65% pure, free of contaminants and chemicals.

My idea was to produce a line of premium omega-3 products—Afinity Cardio Health, Afinity Cognitive Care, Afinity Arthritic Care, and Afinity Omega Health—each targeted to specific conditions.

The goal is a big one, but so much is different this time out. Today, I'm no longer learning how to be a leader, as I was as a young woman in the early nineties when we founded CV and COLD-FX. I have become a natural health product leader. I still have the same ambitious vision: to bring high-quality, high-potency, and pure natural health products to people; to show consumers, through evidence-based research, how they work; and to make a difference in the health and welfare of people.

Although my Afinity brand products will focus on Canada for the time being, I am well aware that within the United States in 2012, the omega-3 fish oil category of products surpassed $2 billion in sales and will continue to grow globally at double-digit rates for a few more years.

As always, I want to show people the science behind my products and provide supporting scientific data, peer-reviewed publications, and white papers to educate key opinion leaders in the pharmacy and medical community—naturopaths, homeopaths, chiropractors, osteopaths, dieticians, nutritionists, and acupuncturists—as well as consumers.

Once my retail distribution is up and running, I will be reaching out to pharmacists as well. I've had experience in this kind of development, and I feel confident my new natural health products will catch people's interest and improve their health. Our past commitment to pharmacy education was important so that pharmacists could play a key role with consumers and their decision-making process.

I never get tired talking about the science behind natural health products because I believe in it. I'm a scientist who grew up in a milieu in which herbal and natural health remedies were part of the generational wisdom handed down, but nonetheless I earned two doctorates in Western medicine, and I feel, deep down, that natural health products are just better for us. I've turned to Western science to perfect and prove my natural health products, and use Western medicine myself when necessary. Like everyone else, I turn to prescription drugs when they are needed, but as much as I am able to do this, I want my own body to stay healthy by taking preventive measures, and by supplementing it with high-quality versions of omega-3 and other natural products that are known to work.

You can see everywhere how interested consumers are in purity these days—many scrutinize every ingredient that goes into their food, many are trying to eat organically and locally. I get excited just thinking of how to contribute my expertise to this demand. Yet this time, I'm being very careful. We learned some valuable lessons with the COLD-FX journey. We will move more slowly into the big U.S. market and other international markets. As many other brands have experienced when they try a U.S. expansion, the market is different there; the American regulatory framework for health-care products presents different challenges than we face in Canada.

So not only am I redefining my own business, I am part of this great group of active agers that is redefining all our expectations about, well, getting old. Don't get me wrong—I am not into cosmetic surgery or trying to look like a teenager. That's why anti-aging seems like a negative term to me, and active aging or even proactive aging seems more positive. I am into glow, energy, vibrancy, vitality, and the self-confidence that comes from just feeling good, within your body and about your body. My mom gave me excellent genes insofar as my outwardly youthful appearance. "Jackie, are you sure you're fifty?" a colleague said to me recently. Oh yes, very sure—I've got the teenage boys, the twenty-five-year marriage, the business resumé, the memories, *and* the worries to prove it!

I am going through my own perimenopause and eventually menopause, but as I have said, it has not always been a graceful or happy time for me. I felt constantly tired, my joints ached, and my moods were all over the place. I am better now with a health-conscious mind and the daily determination to look after myself. Can I find a way for my Afinity Omega-3 products to help women (and men in andropause) navigate this passage gracefully, without resorting to synthetic hormones that can put them at risk for serious conditions? It's that type of question that drives me into the lab every day I can be there, when I can steal some time from the overall demands of running a new business.

As for running that new business, I've learned to be a little more patient. Sometimes, especially in an entrepreneur-driven business, you want something so badly when you're in the building or expanding phase that you see what you want to see. Your passion can cloud your judgement. But risk management is a huge part of managing your business.

So don't do things prematurely. It's easy to say that in hindsight, but not when you're in the middle of something. That comes with experience.

You've got to be open-minded and learn from other people. You need to be able to listen, and not just to correct or praise. You need people who will say no to you and warn you to be cautious. That's very valuable and probably the hardest thing I learned. It's a balancing act—you can't be so cautious that you don't move ahead. A friend in business told me she gets up every day and says to herself, "Always be moving forward." I like that.

7.

# DOING WHAT
# I LOVE TO DO

It was a blustery, rainy fall Saturday in Toronto, and I was
back doing what I love to do—meeting people, selling my
product, educating the public about the science behind my
new Afinity brand. You might remember that in the early
days of the COLD-FX journey, I found myself standing in
an Edmonton Walmart—one of a small group of stores in
the chain that were part of a pilot test. Back then, I was
cheerfully encouraging shoppers to try a then unknown
cold and flu remedy.

Now ten years later, here I was again, selling a new product, with three booths, signs, videos, and many cartons of
my Afinity Omega-3 supplements at the Toronto Zoomers'
show in the massive Direct Energy Centre. The show and
the concept—Zoomers are boomers with zip!—were the
brainchild of media visionary Moses Znaimer, who posed
for a picture with me and congratulated me both for spon-
soring the event and for starting my new company. This was

the sixth annual Zoomer show, and each year, just like our cohort, it has been building in size and momentum.

Standing there in the middle of all the activity, I marvelled at the crowds of active agers strolling through, stopping, and shopping. "Zoom and consume!" read one sign. There were booths that offered them everything from river cruises, to deluxe reading glasses, to digestive aids, to natural health products. Across from me was a psychic, but who had the time to visit her? And besides, I'm a big believer in deciding your own future.

As always I was dressed up—that day I was wearing one of my favourites—a bright rose-coloured jacket, black skirt, and, oh yes, my not exactly comfortable black patent high heels, which I slipped off every chance I could and replaced with my very comfortable flats. I had two speeches to give in which I wanted to highlight the science, purity and quality behind my new line of Afinity omega-3s. And right up to the time I started speaking, I was trying to find the right balance between scientific detail and layman's language to communicate why these products can help so many people with a wide variety of conditions. You know by now that not only am I more comfortable with facts, but I tend to feel more confident sticking to pure science when I am talking about natural health products.

But consumers—especially Zoomers—also wanted a little light-hearted fun along with the practical and scientific insights. Some of them had just participated in a hula hoop fitness class. I needed to grab their attention. First, I rearranged the chairs to suit my style of speaking. Then I delivered my PowerPoint presentation showing diagrams of the potency and purity of omega-3 capsules, and how my company, Afinity, was offering more than 70% purity and potency. I'm a pretty serious person so it might have been not quite the light-hearted moment they were looking for. But I did my best, and business at my booth was brisk. When it comes to natural health products, people always ask a couple of key questions: What will this product do for me? How safe and efficient is it? Consumers also want to know about price, and I was amused by one man who stood in front of me at the Afinity booth, not knowing I was the CEO, and said, with a frown, "Why is this so cheap?" We were offering a special introductory deal that day. That's why.

All of this was and is very personal for me. And fun too. I could spend all day at a trade fair. I believe that if you don't meet the people directly who you are trying to sell to, you can make incorrect assumptions and thus mistakes. You have to stand by and up for your product. You have to be able to answer every question. My goal is to connect, every time out, every way I can. Sometimes I think my fellow scientists look down on me for being so hands-on with the selling, but I really don't care. Scientists can be a very privileged, entitled group of people. They spend all their time in the lab, they even hide in the lab, not just because they love and excel at science, but also maybe because being at a trade show like this would be their idea of public torture. I'm a paradox, I guess. I still spend far more time thinking than I do speaking. I'm still both dreamy and, on the other hand, very passionate and focused about what my company is doing. But for hours at a time, I can just put that creative thinking all aside and on a very personal level just …

relate, educate, and sell. This audience of Zoomers, very educated on their own, tended to ask lots of good questions and seemed to be prevention focused when it came to their health. So I enjoyed connecting with them, helping them understand what is important. Very satisfying for me.

As for long-term goals, we are working on developing three new products in the category of women's health (menopause related), men's health (andropause related), and mental and physical stamina. Very recently, in October 2013, I got back all the technology, patents, and product pipelines other than COLD-FX from Valeant through a licensing agreement. This is great news. It allows us to plan our business in an even longer range, developing products for the treatment of diabetes, cholesterol problems, memory deficiency, even cancer. I have started to dream again.

Wouldn't it be good if the natural health products that other scientists and I produce weren't even labelled as alternative medicine? Right away, that label signals to consumers not to take my product as seriously as prescription medicine, and there is no reason for that. People rely on health-care professionals and caretakers to advise them on how to take care of their health. That means both before and after things go wrong. Mainstream health-care providers need to become more open-minded about natural health products. I believe we're entering a golden age of opportunity and growth for premium quality natural health products. But they have to have proven great therapeutic benefits and be safe and effective. As I recently told the *Globe and Mail,* COLD-FX was probably the most researched and studied product in the natural health industry. That's recognized. The paper was published. You can't deny the research.

Someone asked me recently, "What if you fail?" I don't think that way anymore. I think, "What's the worst thing that could happen? And what if it did?" I've weathered a lot, experienced success, and created something of value that I continue to be very proud of. Success really means different things to different people, and I know what is important to me.

All the hard work and sacrifice has paid off. My health product has not only been tested in the lab and clinical trials, but validated in the real world and by millions of people. What could be more satisfactory? These positive responses and testimonies, which are documented from many consumers, are the fundamental goal for me as a pharmacologist and an entrepreneur. This is what keeps me going even during the darkest, seemingly desperate days (business, bad media publicity, legal issues), and it always pulls me out of even the deepest depression and stressful times, enabling me to get back to what I have been designated to do: developing the best natural medicine so that people can improve their lives.

I talk about efficacy a lot when I talk about my products—they have to be and do what we promise they will do. But in a way I'm also talking about myself. Self-efficacy means using all your skills and ability in every situation, negative or positive, to make things happen. It's not just about high performance, it's about believing you can cause good things to happen, no matter the circumstances. For me, that self-determination started in my childhood, but being in business has convinced me personal efficacy is an indispensable trait.

But yes, like everyone else, I'm a bundle of contradictions. These days I'm working full out, as usual, but trying—trying—to work smarter. My goal is less stress, to be healthy, be happy and be content. I spend a lot of time in my Edmonton home office. Well, actually I have several home offices, which should tell you something. I have a cozy one in the basement, where I hide out a lot in the winter; I have another one on the main floor of the house that overlooks the beautiful Edmonton ravine, so it provides a gorgeous view to inspire me. Occasionally in the summer I make my calls from my patio. And when all else fails, I work in the bedroom!

But I'm also family-centred these days. My boys and I talk a lot, and they even like my cooking. I still like driving them to school and elsewhere after class because it's how we can talk casually about what they want in life and how hard they will have to work to get it. I am all about hard work. "Study your brains out!" I tell them from the driver's seat. "Your brains should be burning." I hear them sigh, but I know they're listening.

Together, Nicholas, Alexander, Eugene, and I go to the gym, and that, along with my weekly hike with girlfriends, keeps me fit. In China, we didn't have gyms or organized sports, but I wasn't very good at them anyway. However it's really important to keep physically strong, especially if,

Hiking in Edmonton River Valley, November 2013. I like to hike with my
girlfriends every weekend.

like me, you're on the road a fair bit. I thought about that recently when I was hiking in the Edmonton Valley with my very fit, very young-looking mom. At seventy-four, she's a wonderful inspiration to me.

As for my daily work life, right now, with a start-up, my focus is mainly on the business side of things. I think as the chief scientific officer, I would be happier spending more time in the lab and that time will come—I am imagining a line of yin and yang products for women and men to help them through the hormonal changes in their lives, and I definitely want to improve people's sleep. I don't get enough sleep myself—I go to bed very late and am miserable if I have to start my day too early. And I really don't want to be stressed, so I—and you, if you're stressed too—have got to find a way to alleviate daily stress.

Being this age is very powerful. You're experienced, you know what could go wrong, but you also are wise enough to know that when things go wrong you can handle it.

If you ask people what they care most passionately about, they tell you they care about their relationships with the people they love, they care about their financial security— especially as they age—and they care about their health. By fifty or so, most of us know that when it comes to our health, certain things are beyond our control—genetics, accidents, the randomness of terminal or serious disease. So why wouldn't we want to control those parts of our health that we can?

When I was in my thirties, I learned how to run. At first, I couldn't do it at all. I'd had respiratory difficulties as a child, and I just didn't seem to have enough breath. But gradually,

I built up enough stamina, and one day I found myself really running hard for an hour and feeling strong and good about it. That was a good day. It was a quiet achievement that mattered only to me.

In business, nothing is ever a solo, let alone a quiet achievement. Certainly any time you start a company and hire people, anything you achieve or fail to achieve matters to far more people than just yourself. I may be the spokesperson and head of my company, but investors, colleagues, my family, and most of all, the people who buy my products because they trust me, matter profoundly in everything that I do. I think about them all and my responsibility to them every day.

I think about who I was, that quiet grad student who arrived without a coat and penniless and never imagined she would still be in Canada more than twenty-five years later. I have a tremendous gratitude to Canada—this country gave me the most precious thing I have—the freedom to create, to think, to innovate, and to grow. Another highlight in my life? I was one of the torchbearers for the relay in the 2010 Vancouver Winter Olympics. In the early morning of October 30, 2010, the first day the Olympic torch arrived in Canada from Greece, I carried the torch. Although I ran for only a short distance, at that moment I was so proud to be a Canadian.

I still can't explain to some people's satisfaction why at fifty, when I could retire or take it easy, I am going for broke with another company. In my first interview with the *Wall Street Journal*, I remember saying it would be such a wonder for me to create a new global health product—and that

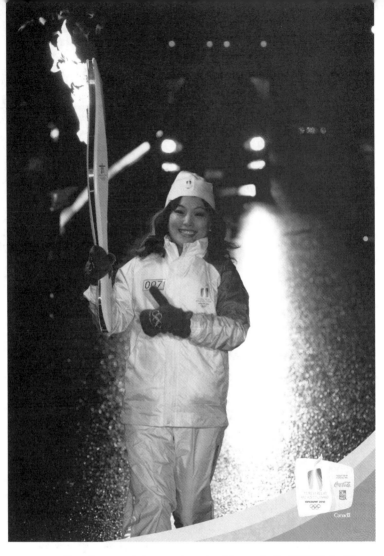

One of my proudest moments as a torch bearer for the 2010 Winter Olympic Games in Canada. In the early morning of October 31, 2010, the Olympic torch relay started in Victoria. I was one of the first torchbearers, wearing number 007.

is still my goal. Other people have suggested that instead of taking on the risk of a new company, I consult or get a government job, although people who know me well know being part of the bureaucracy would drive me crazy.

But something in me wants to be here, right now, taking a risk, but maybe managing it a bit better than last time. The truth is, I love to do exactly what I am doing. Here's another way to think about it. A friend shared with me a great story Hillary Clinton told the audience the last time she spoke in Toronto. She said when her husband's presidency was winding down and she was trying to decide what she would do next, trying to figure out whether she should run for senator, she went to New York as First Lady to hand out an award to a young women's athletic association. As she was on the podium, getting ready to hand out the award, the young recipient came on stage and whispered in her ear. "Mrs. Clinton," she said, "dare to compete." I found that thrilling when I heard it. It spoke to me. Dare to compete.

How ironic. I said I hate to compete, but in my own organic growth and pushing myself to the extreme, all along I was competing. I dared to compete when I was young— becoming an entrepreneur and natural health pioneer instead of staying within the more cloistered walls of the university. That first decade was all about taking my scientific skills and moving into the marketplace, establishing a company and then, as a scientist, spending the better part of ten years researching. The second decade was about commercialization—we came up with a successful product that became a household name in Canada.

And this next decade? Kind of exciting to see what it will bring. A golden age of natural health products? A chance for me to lead more thinking on how we can improve our health by using the best science and an open mind? A decade of active aging for me? That last one I hope is for sure.

Lately I have been thinking of something from early on in the COLD-FX days that still inspires me. We had decided to do a partnership with the Canadian Sport Centre in Calgary, where they train Olympic athletes, and that meant driving to Calgary to meet with them. The day for the drive was September 11, 2001. That's right. I had got up that morning, turned on the television, and watched in horror as the twin towers were attacked, then tumbled down as thousands lost their lives. When I got in the car for the drive, I was still glued to the radio. But once I arrived, I had to put all that darkness aside, and do what I had come to do. One of the athletes training there was Clara Hughes, the Canadian cyclist and speed skater. She had already won several medals by this time, and would win more, becoming one of only four athletes in history to medal at both winter and summer games. As I recall, I met Clara that day and I liked everything about her—her down-to-earth nature, her graciousness, and her generosity. She completely took my mind off all that darkness.

She went on to donate a significant amount of her time and money to Right to Play, an organization that helps disadvantaged youth get into sports, and one that we supported as well. But back in 2001, she was still building toward the height of her achievement and fame. I had heard Clara

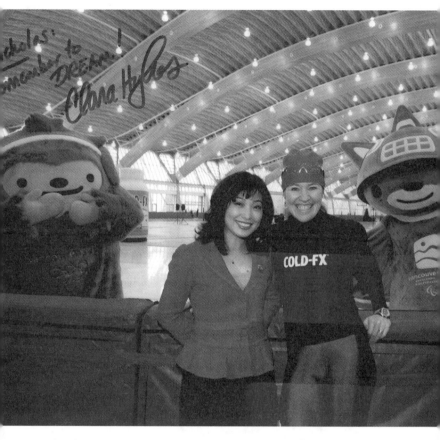

With Clara Hughes prior to the 2010 Winter Olympic Games at the Richmond Olympic Oval. Clara was practising and warming up in this beautiful new Olympic facility. A few days later, I watched her win a bronze medal here in the women's 5000 metres at the age of 39.

loved COLD-FX and so I was delighted when she agreed to help us. Many times after that, when I would watch her train, especially skating, I would be struck by the beauty of what she does as she skates the oval—so focused, so strong, so joyful to watch. Seeing her dedication, her determination to be the best, I felt not only admiration, but inspiration.

When Clara won her last medal in her late thirties, competing with those who were much younger, she inspired awe in me and a bit of envy. *Look*, I thought, *she's not afraid to stand tall with confidence and believe in herself.* I—a very non-athletic scientist—related to her. She had talent, but she also had a strong will. If you want to be the best in your field, you have to have guts and push yourself. It takes courage to go out there. It takes years and years of hard work to win. Clara once signed a picture to my son Nicholas, saying "Remember to dream"!

*Dare to compete. Remember to dream.* They may sound like slogans, but they sum up, almost perfectly, what keeps me going.

8.

# WHAT IT TAKES TO SUCCEED: 24 RULES FOR SUCCESS

Today I love paying special attention to young people—the scientists-to-be, the business-managers-to-be. Whenever I can, I hire young grad students and coach them. I tell them all the time: yes, you *can* do this. They are always so concerned about their futures, never more so than in this highly competitive economy, which in some ways, because of the global financial meltdowns, is far less open than it used to be. I began in very different times. They worry constantly. Will they find work? Will they achieve excellence? Will they make enough money? I tell them the things I would like to have been told at their age—here's how you can get there; here is how you can be a realistic success. What do I mean by realistic success? Success that acknowledges you don't have to be perfect. You just have to try and make the effort every day.

Here's a list of 24 rules for success learned in 25 years. These rules helped me in good times and bad, and I hope will help others.

1.  First rule above all: Work hard. You might not be the most knowledgeable person in the room, but you can work as hard as or harder than anyone else.

2.  Have something on your mind other than making money—a bigger, more worthwhile goal. Mine is creating a successful, respected brand in natural health products that help people and improve their lives. And of course to continue being a natural health pioneer.

3.  Get the most education and training you can, in whatever you choose to do. As I say to my kids, "Study your brains out!" You've got to feel your brain burning until you exhaust every single resource you have.

4.  Listen to the voice that tells you, from within, that you are not giving your all. You are the one person you cannot fool. When you are working flat out, you will know it.

5.  Don't think you have to know everything before you start. I think back to how terrified I was in medical school and even after I graduated, because I thought

I might not know the answer to some obscure problem about anatomy or question about how a drug was constituted. Nobody knows all the answers. Nobody expects you to know all the answers.

6. Finish everything you start. My husband claims I took up sewing as a hobby, made two dresses, and then never went near the sewing machine again. He's right—I decided there were better uses for my time. I'm not a hobby kind of person. That's not my path. But in business and science, if I commit to doing something, I do it until it's done.

7. Rely on yourself as you would a close friend. Be good to yourself. Be proud of your resilience. You're going to need it. Because of the way I grew up, I had to be exceptionally self-motivated and reliant. Today, I am grateful for that. It relates back to that self-efficacy model—the belief that you can cause, make happen, and bring about something good in your life and the lives of others.

8. Choose to be very good at one thing and you will be a success. I tell this to my sons too. You don't have to be a doctor or an engineer. Be what you want to be. But be the very best at it.

9. Never give up. So important for entrepreneurs. Do you think it's easy to go around asking for money? I have scrambled many times for funding. Even today,

as I'm forming a new company, I have to be resourceful. We don't have a lot of cash. And so we are always writing government grant applications. My staff says, "Jackie, we never get these, let's stop after the third go-round." But I say, "Look at the bigger picture and let's go back and back—and back—again."

10. Don't take it personally. I know, everyone says that and then we take a fall and blame ourselves. I did. Or even worse, consider ourselves victims. I did that too. Victims—of a bad management strategy, a crummy economy, circumstances beyond our control. Learn that there's a healthy balance between not blaming yourself and not blaming others, which means accepting responsibility for your role in any situation. People will respect you if you achieve that balance.

11. Don't plan too far ahead—success is more organic than you think. (Amended a bit as I look back and accept that managing risk and assessing future growth means you need to lay down a plan if only to change it.) Don't believe everything the experts tell you—life or business doesn't really unfold in ten-year or even five-year plans. It unfolds at a furious pace, day to day, with problems, challenges, unexpected detours, and surprising successes. Be flexible.

12. Be realistic. I was and am and always will be a dreamer, but because my field was science, I had to be grounded too. One thing about science—when

you do experiments, you fail at least 90% of the time. But mostly it's in the lab, where nobody sees you. One of my biggest challenges? Failing in public. It hurts. But setbacks are a part of growth. I had to learn to be realistic—and resilient about both success and failure.

13. Tomorrow is another day. Thank you, Scarlett O'Hara. When I went through my darkest times in business, I had to tell myself this—and believe it— every single day.

14. Be able to shift your focus. Okay, so one route is blocked. You're not giving up if you find another way through a problem or conundrum even if it looks as though you are abandoning your original idea. This is a creative skill.

15. Always work harder than your employees. It sets a good example and earns you respect. When I started my company in 1992, I was there in the lab before everyone else in the morning, and I turned out the lights at night. It was one of the happiest times in my life.

16. Don't be too hard on yourself. I wish I had been able to have a little more perspective when my business hit a rough patch. I went straight to the f-word: fail-ure. But of course if I had stepped back and looked at the two-plus decades I spent developing a successful

product, the entire arc of my career, I would have felt much better.

17. If there's a job in biotech, take it—seriously, it is a great, innovative, exciting field.

18. Understand that you can learn critical thinking in school, but it's also a character trait. People of real character go through rational steps to solve their problems, both personal and professional. They understand that most problems don't get solved overnight. They act with courage and strength to solve them.

19. Think out loud. Listen quietly. Involve other people who have the skills you don't, experts who may admire what you do but who can help you do it better. People who will say no to you, when you need to hear it.

20. Small but key: If you have a home office, always have a backup computer and printer. Have two. Nothing makes me crazier than technology glitches.

21. If you're a woman, notice who ignores you in a room but don't dwell on it. Find a way of speaking up and contributing that will make everyone stop and listen.

22. If you have to turn someone down—for a job or for some collaborative request—don't just say no, explain why. I wish more people had done that with me when

they turned us down for investments or business deals. I would have learned something.

23.   Listen to your heart about what kind of work makes you happy. Science may have scared me, but it always made me happy. I felt that joy every single day.

24.   The surefire way to guarantee good relationships in business: be authentic. Be what you are, work on the best qualities and skills you have, do not pretend to be what you are not. Others may not be able to describe it, but they know authenticity when they see it. Be the real one in the room.

Epilogue

# TO CHINA,
# WITH LOVE
# (AND TWO BOYS)

In July 2013, in the midst of getting my new company up
and running, I went back to China for two weeks. My husband and I had decided that Nicholas and Alex—then fifteen and eleven—were ready to get to know their heritage.
I wanted them to see everything—where we were born,
where we studied, what China was like as a country. Since I
left so many years ago, China has become somewhat more
open and a world force. I wanted our sons to be proud of
their heritage, and proud of us, too. I visit China every year,
but it's usually on business, with no time to sightsee. So this
was a meaningful trip for all of us.

We flew into Beijing, where my husband's mom lives, so
that was our first stop. She had never met Alex. Apart from
seeing their grandmother, my sons were not impressed—it

was too hot, the streets were narrow and crowded—so crowded—and their first instinct was to say "Let's go home."

But gradually, they began to enjoy this trip down their parents' memory lane. There was the Chinese Academy of Medical Science where their mom had studied—now an ancient building, dwarfed by high-rises everywhere, right near windswept Tiananmen Square. How could I convey to them what a happy time of my life that had been? As a graduate student, I'd had more freedom than I ever had before, and I was studying what I loved. "Okay, Mom" was their typical boy response. *Yawn.* What they really loved was the Beijing Zoo.

After Beijing, we flew to my hometown, Jiujiang—now a metropolitan area of about 4 million. When I was growing up, it had been a city of about 300,000. There in Jiujiang, they met loads of relatives—aunties, uncles, cousins, most of whom they had never met, who treated my boys like little princes. The natural beauty of my hometown, the beauty I had responded to as a daydreaming little girl, was still every-where in evidence—and finally they were impressed. So was I. Somehow the water system had been rebuilt and a dam had created a beautiful lake with little islands. It looked so exotic. My brother Kai—Uncle Kevin to my sons—took them fishing. All my relatives lived in very bright, clean, comfortable homes. The poverty I remembered as a child—small and crowded living conditions, no electricity or toilets—was a thing of the past. I was impressed by how comfortably many people lived.

How can I say this without bragging? I'm pretty famous in my hometown. I took the kids by my old high school,

With family in Jiujiang in 1974. *From left to right*. *Front*: me, sister Ping, brother Kai. *Back*: Dad, Grandma, and Mom.

where in the school museum, they have my picture up, along with the story of my life. I don't know what it meant to my sons—another "Okay, Mom"?—but it meant so much to me to show them.

My childhood called to me everywhere—the apartment where I did most of my daydreaming is still there. I saw some childhood friends. They are so accomplished now. I am in awe of this modern place. And yet my hometown is still very ancient—two sides of the same coin.

What is it about being fifty? You start to care so much for things of the past, you remember so many things dear to you, and yet everything has changed. I can't say it was better back then—especially because China is so different now. The people I know—their lives have been changed for the better. In Jiujiang, even the poorest of people I saw now have shelter and electricity and infrastructure. The grassroots economy has become better, thanks to free enterprise. So I'm very grateful to see that my own relatives have a better life today.

I have never regretted coming to Canada—I made a good choice, and I'm very grateful for that. But sometimes I wonder, *What would have happened to me, what would Xiao Jie have become had she never left China? Would I have been street-smart enough, with enough fortitude and political savvy to climb to the top?* Some of my friends did. Maybe I would have too.

It's very confusing to me. But that confusion is part of the immigrant experience. I carry that confusion of two cultures, a "before" and an "after," everywhere I go.

My husband left us in Jiujiang to go back to Beijing early and see the rest of his family. The boys and I made our way back to Beijing later and then back to Canada. Heading from Beijing to Edmonton on the plane, I felt very relaxed. "This was such a wonderful trip," I told my sons (and not just because they'd behaved so well!). It had made me so happy to show them both the old China—their mom and dad's childhood home—and the new. "We should definitely come back here again," I said to them as the plane took off.

Their response made me smile. "Right now, Mom, we just want to go home." I realized that I did too.

A whole new chapter and a brand-new company were waiting.

# Acknowledgements

I used to imagine that walking down memory lane was something I'd do when I was in the latter part of my life, perhaps on my deathbed. Therefore, it was not easy to start the process of writing down the memories and reflections when we started just a year ago. What a process! Reluctant at the beginning to make it a priority, I found myself drawn more and more to the process, and eventually the floodgates of memory opened. I found it therapeutic, although sometimes painful. At the end, I felt an enormous gratitude toward life and the people in my life. This gratification is extremely powerful, positive, and therapeutic. I am so glad that I have gone through this process now and not waited until on my deathbed!

I hope that in these pages my gratitude is evident toward the people who helped shape my life, career, business, and science. But I also have to say it here, out loud and clear:

To China, my motherland, for giving me a wonderful heritage, culture, and education.

To Canada, my adopted country, for welcoming me with open arms, giving me an education, freedom, and the opportunities to be a scientist and entrepreneur.

To my teachers in China, Professor Zhengang Wang, Professor Yinchang Jing, and Professor Jingsheng Liu, for training me and helping me lay the foundation for being a pharmacologist.

To my mentor, Dr. Peter Pang, for training me, opening the door, and encouraging me as an entrepreneur. COLD-FX was as much your pride and joy as it is mine. I wish we could have written this book together, but you have gone to heaven way too early.

To my long-term trusted colleagues and friends: Gordon Tallman, Dr. Lei Ling, Mike Tallman, Norman Oliver, Dr. Vinti Goel, Dr. Ting Wong, Dr. Tara Lysechko, and Dr. Angela Keuling for your support. Your loyalty and talents made our journey—not one but two business ventures—together much easier and meaningful. Gord, you are a very special chairman to me. Thank you for believing in me and being my most enthusiastic cheerleader and investor who always lifted my spirit and confidence when needed. You are a role model—highly principled, with great integrity, and great respect for life. I learned and will continue to learn a great deal from you in business and in life.

I want to thank again the people who supported me and COLD-FX: Clara Hughes, Don Cherry, Mark Messier, Paul Rosen, and the Edmonton Oilers; you are sources of inspiration and symbols of never giving up. I would like to thank you and the following people for giving me permission to publish the "you and me" pictures representing the fond memories and moments that I treasure: Prime Minister Stephen Harper, Margaret Atwood, Mayor Stephen Mandel, Iris Evans, Bill Comrie.

To our science and clinical collaborators, Dr. Janet McElhaney, Dr. Gerry Predy, Dr. Tapan Basu, Dr. Sandra

Miller, Dr. Ken Rosenthal, Dr. Andrew Simor, for helping us advance our scientific vision and reaching many important scientific milestones.

To my scientific and management team in last twenty years, what can I say? You are like family to me, and without you I would have had no story to tell. We have gone through ups and downs together in that long COLD-FX journey. I won't list the names for fear of missing any. But I would like to thank you particularly, Dr. Sharla Sutherland, for working side by side with me, sharing the heavy loads, sometimes a heavy heart, with me during those difficult times, for organizing and handing me the statue of a phoenix and the memorable collage album containing all the good wishes and pictures from our team in the last few days in the COLD-FX building.

To all my supporting investors and users of COLD-FX, I can't thank you enough. I want to thank the angel investors who helped in the early days. You are my true believers! With your recognition and validation, my dream has come true.

To my longtime advisors Dr. Bob Church, Ted Bilyea, David Wayne, David Weyant, and Doug Gilpin, thank you for supporting me and providing your wise counsel to me and my team in both ventures.

I would like to thank the funding agency and organizations NRC/IRAP and AVAC for their contribution to and investment in both our ventures. These organizations help advance life science innovation and entrepreneurs in Canada. We need more of them.

I would like to thank Judith Timson, the award-winning journalist and author, for helping me bring my story to life.

Our endless conversations and changing notes have been therapeutic to me and have helped me gain more confidence in relating my journey.

To Sarah Scott, my excellent and timeline-pressed publisher, thank you for showing me the publishing world of business. Your diligent project managing has made the book a reality.

To Mom and Dad, thank you for giving me life, raising me, and giving me unconditional love. Dad, I know you are watching over and protecting me from heaven. I want to let you know that I miss you so much.

To my brother Kai and sister Ping, I am so grateful to have you as family. Like Mom and Dad, I can always count on your unconditional love and support no matter what.

To my first-born Nicholas, on the day you were born, I felt my life was completed. You taught me life is not just about deadlines, meetings, and business. You have finally made me realize that you will definitely not be starving if you don't become a doctor, an engineer, or accountant someday. To my younger son, Alex, thank you for being so understanding and supportive of Mom's business. I still have the first draft of the Afinity logo you helped design. I was so proud that you helped sell the first batch of Afinity brands on Afinity's launching day. Who knows—someday you may want to be a scientist or entrepreneur. Nicholas and Alex, I love you to pieces.

And last, but not the least, to my husband, Yuejiun (Eugene), thank you for being there for me, for better and worse. You are my rock. When all else fails, we always have each other.

# About the Author

Jacqueline Shan founded her second life science company, Afinity (Afinix) Life Sciences Inc. (www.afinity.ca), in January 2012, after the sale of Afexa Life Sciences Inc., a company she co-founded. She is the president, CEO, and chief scientific officer. Both companies focus on the business of development and commercialization of evidence-based natural health products.

Dr. Shan is the co-founder of Afexa Life Sciences Inc. (formally CV Technologies Inc.), a biopharmaceutical company spun off from the University of Alberta in 1992. She helped the company set its original vision: to be the leader in discovering, developing, and commercializing evidence-based polymolecular botanical medicines. Since then, Dr. Shan has established a portfolio of technology platforms, IPs, and product pipelines for the company while developing an extensive network of laboratory and clinical collaboration programs with national and international organizations in both academic and industrial sectors.

From 2003 to 2008, Dr. Shan served as the president, CEO, and chief scientific officer of Afexa. She led the company in an aggressive commercialization plan, which resulted in product regulatory approval, phenomenal brand awareness, and sales growth (to more than $40 million in

Canada) of its flagship product, COLD-FX, which she co-discovered. It has been the number-one-selling and number-one pharmacist-recommended cold and flu remedy in Canada every year since 2005. In 2009, Dr. Shan stepped down as CEO but remained as chief scientific officer. After Afexa Life Science Inc. was acquired by Valeant Pharmaceutical Inc. in 2011, Dr. Shan left Valeant/Afexa and founded another Alberta-based life science company, now called Afinity Life Sciences Inc. It develops and commercializes biopharmaceutical and other life science–related products.

Dr. Shan is the first and only female CEO who founded and listed her company on the TSX in health care, life sciences, and consumer goods and has received more than twenty-five national and international awards in both business and science, including the Alberta Centennial Medal from the premier of the province in recognition of outstanding service to the people and the province of Alberta. She has been recognized three times as one of Canada's 100 Most Powerful Women by the Women's Executive Network. She has also been recognized as one of Canada's 50 Most Powerful Women by *Profit* magazine, and as a Woman of Vision by Global Television. She also received a Best of Best of Chinese-Canadian Entrepreneurs award from the Chinese Canadian Business Association. Dr. Shan has been inducted into the Canadian Pharmaceutical Industry Hall of Fame and has been the cover story in more than ten science and business magazines in Canada.

In 2009, Dr. Shan was appointed by the Minister of Advanced Education and Technology to the Alberta Innovates—Bio Solutions board of directors. Dr. Shan has been an advisory board member for Small- and Medium-sized Enterprises (SME), International Trade of Ministry of Foreign Affairs, since November 2010, and was previously a founding board member of the Alberta Life Sciences Institute, appointed by the Alberta government. In addition to her directorship for BioAlberta (the industry association for Alberta's biotechnology and life sciences industry), she is a member of A100 and was a member of the Strategic Advisory Board for the Institute of Infection, Immunity and Inflammation at the University of Calgary.

Dr. Shan has been a visiting professor at the Chinese Agriculture University, Professor Adjunct at the University of Alberta; Distinguished Visiting Investigator at the National Research Institute of Chinese Medicine in Taiwan; Visiting Professor at the Peking Union Medical College/Chinese Academy of Medical Sciences; and Visiting Associate Professor at the University of Hong Kong. In 2013, she was WEConnect certified, which supports supplier diversity initiatives with women-led enterprises, and is a 2014 (AWE) Alberta Women Entrepreneur nominee. Dr. Shan has authored and co-authored more than sixty peer-reviewed scientific papers and is co-inventor of more than forty U.S. and PCT (Patent Cooperation Treaty) patents.

Dr. Shan holds a Ph.D. in physiology from the University of Alberta and a Doctor of Science in pharmacology from the Chinese Academy of Medical Sciences/Peking Union Medical College, is certified by the Quantum Shift Program (Executive Business and Entrepreneurship) from the Richard Ivey Business School, and holds ICD.D (Institute of Corporate Directors) accreditation.